SMUDGEPOT

A TRIUMPH OF LOVE
OVER CANCER

JOHN M DIVIGGIANO

ISBN-13: 978-1484830352

ISBN-10: 1484830350

Library of Congress Cataloging-In-Publication Data Available

Book Design by: John M. DiViggiano

Printed in the United States of America

Library of Congress Control Number: 2013911946
CreateSpace Independent Publishing Platform
North Charleston, South Carolina

DEDICATION

I would like to dedicate this book to Dr. Rosalind Catchatourian, Dr. Margaret Telfer, and Anita Bontuyan, Clinical Nurse Specialist. Mary lived for nearly eighteen years after her diagnosis of non-Hodgkin's lymphoma because of their medical knowledge and expertise. Their compassionate care, combined with cutting-edge medical technology, was the reason why Mary lived past the standard seven-to-ten-year prognosis.

These three remarkable women bonded with Mary and quickly gained my confidence and admiration. The five of us were a team, fighting a life-threatening illness, and leaving no stone unturned to conquer it. In the end, although Mary lost the battle, she was able to live a rich and fulfilling life.

I would be remiss if I did not mention the contribution of the nation's pharmaceutical companies, whose research and development create the miracle drugs that treat blood-related cancers.

It is customary to thank individuals who helped an author pen a book. Mary, I thank you and bless the day I walked into your office. You made me deliriously happy, proved that I could love and be loved, and made me the man that I am. I am a better person for having known you…more confident and self-assured and closer than ever to my family. I now look at life with a sense of wonder. You taught me how to be brave in the face of a frightening illness and how to accept the things I can't change—but only after giving it one hell of a fight.

PREFACE

In the course of grieving the loss of my beloved wife, Mary, I decided that I needed to put my thoughts and feelings into print. I thought that writing about this extraordinary woman and our wonderful life together would be a difficult and sometimes painful process. But it was one that I had to see to completion, no matter what emotions it evoked. To my surprise, as I retold her many colorful stories, I smiled and laughed more than I cried. When I cried, it was mostly over things that will never be: trips that we'll never take, advice we'll never give each other, and her physical presence that is gone forever.

Instead of focusing on what I've lost, this book has helped me reflect on what I had for more than twenty-six years with Mary. I am the luckiest man in the world to have known and been loved by Mary Charlotte Kasper DiViggiano. Friends have told me that many people never find the true love we shared, that ours was a truly special relationship. It was indeed.

There will never be another Mary Charlotte, except for the girl who lives in my heart and mind, and with whom I have forged a new relationship that will last for eternity.

CONTENTS

1

Angel's Paradise

LIFE ON THE FARM

In 1945, Joe C. Kasper wasn't thinking about farming, hogs, or his boyhood home in Morse, Iowa. He was busy fighting the Japanese army in the Philippine islands of the South Pacific. It was a memorable year: FDR died; my uncle, Edward J. Moskala was killed on Ryukyu Ridge in Okinawa, earning the Congressional Medal of Honor; and Joe Kasper's bullet wound in his arm got him an early ride back to Iowa. That wound gave him a lifelong disability check, but never interfered with his golf game later in life. I wouldn't often play with my father-in-law because—despite his war wound, two artificial knees, and terrible form—he was a scratch golfer who played every day. When I did play with him, he would, in typical Joe fashion, describe my worst shot as, "a damn good effort," or "You got the makin's, boy." He was your biggest fan, your favorite high school coach, and your own built-in motivational trainer. In other words, he was one great dad to my Mary Charlotte and her sisters.

Once home from the war, Joe went back to the occupation of his father, farming the fertile land of Iowa. In 1946, he had the good fortune to attend an Iowa Democratic Party fund-raising dance at the Czechoslovak Hall in Iowa City one Saturday night. There, he caught the eye of Amelia Amelon, a single woman of German descent who was unmarried at thirty-five, and probably wrestling with her biological clock. She asked her friend, "Who's that handsome man in the brown suit?" The friend replied, "Why that's Joe Kasper, just back from the war; he farms in Johnson County." Joe didn't know it at that moment, but despite the Bell's palsy that plagued him since his childhood, Amelia thought he was the most attractive man in the hall that night.

Mel (pronounced *meal*) was quite the independent woman. She lied about her lack of a high school diploma in order to enter the Irish Business School, and earned a secretarial certificate (though she was not proud that she lied, and made it clear that it was wrong). She was also one of the first women in Iowa City to own her own car, a green Willys Roadster with a rumble seat. A "townie," she lived in Iowa City and worked as a clerk for the town's mayor. She was one of five children, with three brothers and a spinster sister, Leona, who was a key figure in Mary's early years.

Joe and Mel were married in 1946 and started having babies right away. Their first was born in 1947. Later in life, Carolyn Ann would take on the looks and characteristics of her grandma Charlotte "Lottie" Kasper— tall, thin, and introspective. Joe nicknamed Carolyn Ann "Main Spoke" because she was the first. This nicknaming became SOP (standard operating procedure) for Joe when each of their children was born. The next one to come along was the subject of this book, Mary Charlotte Kasper, who he promptly nicknamed "Smudgepot" because of the shock of dark hair she sported at birth. Next came Phyllis Jean in 1950, known to him as "Slicko" for her lack of hair at birth. She was the sensitive one who, as a little girl, cried when she accidently sat on her pet kitten and killed it. Mel lost a child after Phyllis was born, but was soon blessed with their last daughter Jane Amelia in 1951. Joe nicknamed her "Torpedo" because of her knack for taking on a job and ramming it through to completion (I suspect this nickname came later).

People joked because, as hard as he tried, Joe Kasper could not produce a farmhand—aka a son. Life on the farm near Solon, Iowa, was idyllic for those four little girls. Mary speculated that Mel kept them on the plump side to discourage the boys, but that probably had more to do with a 1950s era mom encouraging her kids to clean their dinner plates because there were kids starving in China! Mel happened to be an accomplished seamstress who made all of their clothes and, despite Joe's best efforts, was determined to raise ladies. Whenever a tornado threatened, Mel would herd the girls into the cellar and stand over the washtubs, lighting palms with her Camel cigarette and reciting the Lord's Prayer. There was always a carton of unfiltered Camels on top of the refrigerator in their 1950s rural kitchen.

Joe had a rather colorful vocabulary, in which the word *goddamned* played prominently. Some might think it was using the Lord's name in vain, but to him and to most of us, it was an endearing manner of speech. Joe would come out of church and remark, "That was a goddamned good sermon." Expletives played prominently in Joe's vocabulary, but that was as much a part of farm life as driving a tractor. Rest assured, Joe is adding color to heaven right now with his down-home manner of speaking.

A tractor was the first vehicle Mary learned to drive, as it was for many farm kids in the fifties. (Even now, in rural communities in Iowa, adolescents can get their learner's permit at fourteen.) Mary told me the story of how, as a young girl, she once drove the tractor with her dad standing on the rear platform. Suddenly she looked back and he was gone. There he was, standing in the field behind her waving as she drove solo for the first time. She would ride out to the fields with her dad to look at the herd. If the cattle ate too much clover, they would bloat with gas, and it could be fatal, so Joe would go out to the fields and look for animals that were in trouble. He would walk up to the afflicted bovine and plunge a knife into its bloated belly, thereby releasing the buildup of gas. Being a city boy, I was appalled when Mary told me that story, but I have been assured that it was a common practice in the fifties, and despite its gruesome nature, the best thing for the animal. Joe was not above telling the girls to fill a feed sack or pitchfork some hay, but when it came time to cut the hogs (castrate them) or for them to farrow (give birth), the girls were not allowed to watch; Mel made sure of that.

Believe it or not, Mary had a little lamb. Its name was Mutton, and it was probably one of the lambs they had incubated in the kitchen oven when it was first born. Mutton was Mary's pet until the day it ate Mel's forsythia bush. Then Mutton ran away, or at least that's what Mary was told. Mary's other pet was a black mare which she named Sugar. (It is interesting to note that as a boy I had a black Labrador Retriever-Collie mix that I named Sugar. Is it any wonder that we were meant to be together?) Mary would ride Sugar on her dad's acreage, and was fond of a stand of timber next to the creek. She named this place Angel's Paradise. It was there that she would spend hours living in a little girl's world of make-believe, probably dreaming of her knight in shining armor. She told me many times that I was that person, and every time she spoke of Angel's Paradise, there was a gleam in her eye.

Mary's childhood was deliriously happy, and she was surrounded by love and affection. Even though Mel was the disciplinarian and not prone to spontaneous displays of affection, she was a loving mother who was dedicated to her girls and instilled in them her faith in God, respect for nature and people, her talents as a seamstress, and showed them how to be a strong, independent, and productive woman who loved her husband. Joe was probably not the most successful farmer, and he loved to drink beer, but he knew how to have fun, and that made an indelible impression on Mary. There wasn't a time when Joe didn't wrestle with his girls, give them sloppy kisses, and—to Mel's horror—sing off-color songs to them, like "Has Anyone Seen My Gal?" Unlike my dad, there wasn't an ice cream stand that Joe would pass by without stopping, and when the Iowa Hawkeye's were playing, they all crowded in front of the radio as Joe did the play-by-play. Joe Kasper, the man with four daughters, had a basketball hoop hanging on the barn. In the winter, he and the girls would play fox and goose in the snow and make snowmen in the front yard.

One of Mary's fondest memories was of one particular Christmas Eve when she was just a little girl. Santa always arrived at the Kasper farm on Christmas Eve, so one year Joe rigged up some buckets on the front porch with a string attached to them. The string ran up through a window and to his chair at the dining room table. Just as they finished dinner, Joe yanked on the string, sending the buckets crashing down. He jumped up and said, "What's that racket out there; it must be Santa!" The four girls ran out the front door to find all of their Christmas gifts strewn in the snow in the front yard. Mary would tell that story as though it happened yesterday.

She loved her dad dearly, and, as a little girl, never missed an opportunity to hold his hand. One day while in town, she was holding her daddy's hand, but because he was preoccupied with something, he shook her off and said, "You have to go it on your own, little peggler," She promptly cried. Years later, as she and I were walking through Stow-On-The-Wold in the English Cotswolds, I wouldn't hold her hand because I was busy taking pictures or just feeling standoffish that day. She pouted all day while we visited Lake Windermere in the English Lake District. That look became known as the Windermere Pout, and we laughed whenever I mentioned it. Mary's connection to her dad was deep, real, and carried over into our married life. In some ways, I took over for Joe, the protector, the guidance counselor, the cheerleader, the loving man.

Mary was also close to her cousins who lived in nearby Morse, Iowa, and in Lincoln, Nebraska. When all the cousins were in town, it was a "girl fest," complete with sleepovers, rides on Sugar, camping, and that most memorable (and illegal) of family activities—fish trapping on the Cedar River. Oh, yes, it was illegal to set traps for catfish in Iowa. Joe and his brother John, and hundreds of other Iowa farmers, routinely set large, wire fish traps and enjoyed bountiful catches of the tasty, however ugly, freshwater fish. They used a special stink bait that they purchased somewhere in Muscatine, Iowa, a historic river town on the Mississippi. The bait was old scrapings from a cheese factory, and it stunk to high heaven. But the worse the smell, the better it worked. Joe always told the story of how he and John went to buy some and forgot it was in the trunk of the car—probably after having a beer or two. Days later, a decomposing body could not have smelled as bad. Anyway, the girls would accompany Joe and John to the river around midnight. They would sneak through the weeds and reeds, shushing each other so the game warden wouldn't hear them. They'd check the traps and empty them when needed, throwing the big whiskered fish into the pickup bed. Mary always remarked that they made a sucking sound as they flapped their gills. As the family retreated to the truck, they would groom the reeds so it would not look like they'd been there. It was all so clandestine, and a whole lot of fun.

Joe liked beer. Who didn't? It was the drug of choice for that generation, my dad's included. When Joe would sell some hogs, it was time to celebrate at the Morse General Store, which also had a bar with a brass rail. Mary remembered going there with her dad and sitting on the brass rail while drinking a grape Nehi. She recalled the time a neighbor got drunk and rode his horse right up the steps, through the door, and into the bar.

Cousin Susan talked about the time she was in from Lincoln visiting Uncle John and Aunt Mag, and decided to ride into Solon with Uncle John. She was probably six years old and content to sit in the pickup while Uncle John went inside the local tavern. Hours went by until Joe appeared and asked, "Where's Uncle Jack?" She pointed to the bar and said she'd been waiting for hours. "Don't you fret, little one; I'll go get him for you," said Joe. Susan fell asleep while waiting for both her uncles to come out—well past sunset.

For a time, Joe drove cattle to the Union Stock Yards in Chicago. Mary remembered how her dad and mom would come to school and pull them out to go on a road trip. I guess they did that when they heard the current price of cattle on the radio. They routinely listened to the farm reports by Orion Samuelson on WLS out of Chicago. In the 1950s, the Chicago Stock Yards bustled with activity. Mary recalled vividly the looks, the smells, and the excitement of being there. On one occasion, a bull got loose from its pen and stampeded through the corrals. She remembers a large man scooping her up and placing her high atop a fence as the raging bull sped by her. One of her childhood "knights in shining armor," no doubt.

The family's farm was in rural Solon, but there was no bus service to Solon, so it was decided that the kids would go to school in West Branch. Mary's bus ride was about the longest because of where she lived, and much of it was on gravel roads, so there's no telling how much road dust she ingested daily. West Branch has historical significance because it was the boyhood home of Herbert Hoover, and is now the site of his grave and presidential library. At the burial of President Hoover in 1964, Mary sang at his graveside with the school choir. She was always proud about that.

One day in kindergarten Mary came up behind a little girl whose bow had come untied on the back of her little dress. Mary tied that bow and began a lifelong friendship with Linda Marie. Word has it that Linda Marie was quite the looker back in high school, but very aloof when it came to boyfriends. One boy remarked that kissing Linda Marie was like kissing a doorknob, "At least as hard and twice as cold."

Mary did not have problems with boys because she was on the chubby side. (Mary subsequently struggled during much of her life with a weight problem, especially in her young adult years). Her prom date was Dennis, her sister Phyllis's boyfriend and now her husband. He came in handy when one of the other girls needed an escort. Joe wanted Mary to marry Billy Joe because his folks had a lot of farmland, and Billy Joe had a boat. Mary speculated that Joe wanted the boat, and not much else. Mary always likened herself and Billy Joe to Jack Sprat and his wife because Billy Joe was tall and lanky, and wore high-water pants. I don't know what happened to Billy Joe, but I'm guessing he's a millionaire landowner and may still have that boat.

Joe built a boat once, then realized that he couldn't get it out of the cellar. He finally did, and named it the *CaMaPhaJa,* after Carolyn, Mary, Phyllis, and Jane. It was a flat-bottom fishing boat that came in handy when setting those catfish traps on the Cedar River.

Mary was an exemplary student and was inducted into the DAR. Quite frankly, I'm not sure why membership in the Daughters of the American Revolution was such a distinction, but she was proud of it nevertheless. Life at West Branch High School was always a fond memory for Mary. She spoke with great affection about classmates Karen ("Kay-Kay"), Clifford ("Cliffy"), Andrew ("Andy"), Bruce, and, of course, her best friend Linda Marie. Mary was active in school activities and even starred in a school play or two, such as *Brigadoon.* Her PE coach was a relative of Dennis'. Mary fondly remembered "Jumpin'" Jenny, and actually had contact with her at certain family functions in recent years.

Mary was not athletic, but she loved to watch and support the West Branch Bears. After we married, we relished every opportunity to see our nephews play football and baseball for the Bears. We'd also enjoy watching our niece Annie pretend to play the trombone in the marching band; we could see that she was simply puffing her cheeks rather than playing for real.

Some of Mary's fondest memories were of her sleepovers at Linda Marie's house. Linda's father, Delbert, was a farmer who had given up life on the farm and moved his family to town in West Branch. His wife, Marjorie, worked for the telephone company and Delbert stayed at home, read books, and probably had a drink or two. Mary said Delbert was always good for an excuse note when the girls decided to be late or ditch school.

7

SMUDGEPOT

The graduating class of 1966 numbered sixty homegrown, mainstream, genuinely good kids who loved their parents, were fiercely proud of their school, probably drank a beer or two, and to this day gather every ten years to get together and reminisce. Mary made every reunion, except for their fortieth, and that was because she had been diagnosed with myelodysplastic syndrome and needed to begin treatment in an attempt to save her life.

I accompanied Mary to one of her class reunions shortly after we met. As we drove to Dubuque, Iowa, to board a dinner cruise on a Mississippi River paddle wheeler—with Linda Marie in the backseat—Mary proceeded to flip down the glove compartment door of my brand new Cadillac Coupe Deville and began to polish her nails. I never said a word about it until several years later when I remarked, "Don't you EVER do your nails in my car again!" That was a waste of breath because she simply replied, "Oh, piffle!"

2

The Mad Hatter

AUNT LEONA

All of Amelia Amelon's siblings got married except for Leona, and all would suffer from emphysema later in life. It is a devastating disease that is exacerbated, if not caused by, cigarette smoking. All of the Amelons smoked, Amelia and Leona included, but it ended Leona's life much sooner in the 1970s. Having never met Aunt Leona, I can only relate things that Mary shared with me about this memorable woman.

Aunt Leona was a spinster who lived with her mother and ran a tearoom in downtown Iowa City. It was called The Mad Hatter, and was on the second floor in a building at 124-1/2 Iowa Avenue, in the heart of the downtown college district. Mary remembered going there as a little girl and had a sugar and creamer set from the place.

Even today, when I stand across the street and look at that building on Iowa Avenue, I look up and can picture a very young Mary Charlotte Kasper sitting in the window, gazing at the world below. I can only imagine what was going on in that little girl's head. I suspect the travel bug bit her at an early age, and she was already thinking about the places in this

9

wonderful world she'd like to see. I have a feeling her Aunt Leona's bohemian spirit was bestowed upon Mary. Although Leona led a provincial life, she inspired Mary to experience everything. Leona had a collection of old 78 rpm records, which fostered Mary's love of piano and classical music. Mary once told me the story of how she would sit and listen to Chopin for hours on end until one day she accidentally dropped the record and it shattered on the floor. She cried and cried because she thought she'd never get to hear that beautiful music again.

Leona never married, but she had a male boarder named George, and it was always whispered that Leona and George were an item. I suppose the neighbors had their opinions, but no one in the family seemed to care. Her life's ambition was to help her sister Amelia raise ladies. This Victorian-Age-minded woman taught the Kasper girls manners: how to set a table, how to dress appropriately..."scarves before noon and pearls after five," and Mary's favorite, "always wear a hat to an afternoon wedding." Mary adopted Aunt Leona's taunt, "Who's your friend Mian?" which was a sarcastic way of responding to an improper phrase like, "Me and Dan are going to the movies." One of Leona's biggest pet peeves was when a person ended a sentence with a preposition, such as, "Where are you staying at?" Mary unconsciously emulated her aunt every time she corrected her nieces' and nephews' grammar.

Leona would haunt me as well. When Mary and I had dinner parties at our home in Palos Park, Illinois, I was always corrected by the ghost of Aunt Leona (channeled through Mary) when I did not position the silverware properly...one inch from the edge of the table. As annoying as Aunt Leona may have been to those four little Kasper girls, she made a huge impact on Mary that stayed with her and influenced others—myself included—long after Leona drew her last breath. It's amazing how an influential person, however annoying at the time, can enrich your life and make you proud.

Somehow, I think Mary has had a similar impact on her seven nieces and nephews. They know how annoying she could be, but also how loving she was, and I know they cherish every moment they spent with her. Mary had a habit of calling each kid at the crack of dawn on his or her birthday. They'd say, "Aunt Mary, I'm still sleeping." She'd reply, "That's okay, you're up now, so let's talk. What's going on in your life?" Mary had a favorite quote by Louisa May Alcott that is still taped to the inside of her address book, it reads: "Fatherly and motherly hearts often beat warm and wise in the hearts of bachelor uncles and maiden aunts; and it is my private opinion that these worthy creatures are a beautiful provision of nature for the cherishing of other people's children."

As sick as Mary was from the chemotherapy over the last eighteen years, when it came to those seven nieces and nephews, she rarely missed a chance to be at a football game, recital, or graduation. She would often share pearls of wisdom with them. As she once said to Annie, "Your body is a temple, and only a select few should be allowed to worship!"

Few people can say they had an aunt who cared as much about them... or an uncle who just may continue the crack-of-dawn birthday phone calls.

3

Stub

THE UNIVERSITY OF IOWA

For Mary, college was a foregone conclusion when she was growing up on the farm. Joe graduated from Solon High School, but Mel did not, and they were determined that their girls would have more in life. I'm not sure how well educated Aunt Leona was, but being Mel's sister, I'll guarantee she reinforced the idea of getting a college degree.

I must say the Kaspers were far more forward thinking than the DiViggianos. My siblings and I were encouraged to finish high school and learn a trade. My dad was a truck driver, and he was convinced that the big money was in pipefitting, carpentry, masonry, and similar fields. He was not impressed with college graduates, but if a man could lay a brick... that was all right in his book.

All of the Kasper girls graduated from the University of Iowa. In the late 1960s Joe and Mel decided it was time they quit farming and move to town. The fact that their daughters were going to attend school there may have been a factor. To this day, Phyllis has the framed poster announcing the auction held at the farm when Joe was closing out in 1968. Joe and Mel

13

purchased a three-bedroom ranch on Radcliffe Avenue, on the east side of Iowa City. All the girls lived at home when they started at U of I.

The folks were determined to see the girls get their parchment, but hey, they didn't say they were going to pay for it. If I'm not mistaken, they paid for the first year, but after that, the girls were on their own. That meant all sorts of interesting, character-building jobs for Mary, like working the S.S.Kresge & Co. store lunch counter. That job lasted exactly one day, because my Mary needed a bigger challenge. On one occasion, Mary responded to an ad for a secretary and Mel decided to accompany her to the interview. Part of the interview was a typing test in which she had to type the phrase, "The big brown raft turned in the river"; easy enough. Well, she promptly typed out, "The big brown fart turned in the river," and was told that they'd call her. Mary went back to the car where Mel eagerly waited and told her mom what happened. Mel looked her in the eye and said, "You march right back in there and tell them you can do that job." She did, and they hired her. If I ever wondered where Mary got her tenacity and nerve, all I have to do is recall the typing test incident and it brings a huge smile to my face. For all that Joe was, fun-loving, gregarious, and charming, Amelia Kasper was an intelligent thinker, a tough woman who knew that life was no bed of roses, and self-confidence was just as important as skill. We may not know it at the time, but these types of character-building experiences in our youth lay the foundation for who and what we become as adults.

The college job that made the biggest impact on Mary was probably her role as girl Friday to Iowa Football Coach Forest Evashevski. The man was tough as nails and had a colorful vocabulary, making a farmer sound like an altar boy. She recalled how he used to sit in his office, leaning back in his chair with his huge feet propped up on the desk. He'd be barking obscenities at someone on the phone one minute and politely speaking to a group of nuns the next. After twenty-six years with Mary, I can see how some of Mr. Evashevski may have rubbed off on her.

—————

As you can well imagine, Mary had many close friends in college. She was a big hit with the boys, but not because she was the "hot chick." Remember, it was speculated that Joe and Mel kept their girls on the plump side so they wouldn't suffer the fate of some others...pregnancy without the benefit of marriage. That was in the days when a child out of wedlock, or being a pregnant bride, was something to be ashamed of. I remember when an eighth-grade or high school girl got pregnant in a Catholic community, she was whisked away to some special place to complete her term and have the child to give it up for adoption. Back then, there was such a place in Chicago run by Catholic nuns called the Misericordia Home. Similar places still exist today, but unmarried pregnant girls and women are less likely to be sent away to have their children. This is because of all the celebrities who decide that having a child is okay, whether you're single, living together, married to another woman, or simply feel that it's time to make some headlines. There is no shame associated with pregnancy outside of marriage anymore, and we can all thank Hollywood for that. But I digress.

Mary's male friends happened to be a group of guys from Atlantic, Iowa. They were the sons of doctors and attorneys, and all came from backgrounds of privilege and rank. But they shared something with Mary that probably wasn't apparent to them at the time...they knew a college degree was important. One thing that echoes with her former college friends is that "Stub," as Mary was called, was the common thread among them. She was the catalyst that brought them together and the glue that bound them. If there was fun to be had, Mary was the ringleader. Her infectious smile and outgoing personality was intoxicating. I know that because I was captivated the very moment I met her.

College life during the late sixties and early seventies was turbulent and violent at times. Students commandeered some university buildings, demanding an end to the war in Vietnam; burned their bras and draft cards; and basically did all the things that Liberal college students did back then. Kent State was probably the most famous incident of the era, and it deeply impacted Mary and all of her friends. The Ohio National Guard opened fire on Kent State University student protesters, killing several and injuring others. It was an unnecessary and useless waste of young lives during a very tumultuous time in US history. Back in that era, as today, most college kids were Liberals. Being Liberal herself back then, Mary campaigned for Bobby Kennedy and was devastated when he was shot and killed in Los Angeles. She remained a Liberal Democrat until two men entered her life right around 1980: Ronald Reagan and John DiViggiano.

4

Furlough

AROUND THE WORLD ON PAN AM FLIGHT 1

After college, Mary was given an opportunity to move to Richmond, Virginia, and work for Loren and Rita Kotner's travel agency. She did so, but soon moved to Washington, DC, to work in reservations for American Airlines at Dulles International Airport. Travel jobs, especially in the seventies, were ridiculously low paying, so we were always looking for new opportunities. She lived in Alexandria and rode her bicycle down the George Washington Parkway to the airport every day. John Dean, the famous Watergate conspirator lived a few doors down, and Mary was standing at the gates of the White House when Richard Nixon resigned in 1975. She was always proud to say that she was a witness to history back then. Little did she know that nearly thirty years later, she'd be back there shaking hands with President George W. Bush.

The airline industry was volatile in the seventies, and most people expected a furlough, or layoff, eventually. When that furlough came, it wasn't necessarily a bad thing for Mary. She moved back to Iowa City and promptly bought an around-the-world ticket on Pan Am Flight 1 at the airline employee rate of slightly more than $600. Her parents were not exactly overjoyed with the idea that their daughter would want to travel around the world by herself. She assured them that she'd be okay, and set out on her solo journey. She left Cedar Rapids and flew to California to be the maid of honor for her college friend Valorie.

After that, Mary lost touch with Valorie until after we were married, but the two of them rekindled their friendship as if it had never been interrupted. Mary always felt that true friends could do that: lose touch and pick up right where they left off, even years later. Mary had a habit of associating herself with accomplished women. Linda Marie obtained her nursing degree, worked for the Kidney Foundation in Des Moines, and is now a nurse practitioner in Port Hadlock, Washington. Valorie has a law degree and went on to become an associate dean at Clemson University. One of Mary's favorite sayings was, "Women are like tea leaves; you don't know how strong they are until they're in hot water." All of these women have had their trials and tribulations, but the saying holds true, and they have risen above it all.

———

After the wedding, Mary flew to Honolulu and then to Tokyo. She always told the story of how she slept for days, partly because she was too freaked out to come out of her room. After her initial fears abated, she became an avid sightseer who rode the bullet train, walked through Ginza, touched the Giant Daibutsu of Kamakura, and watched a sumo wrestling match.

She continued on to Australia, stopping to see the Sydney Opera House on Sydney Harbor, toured the Great Barrier Reef, and explored the eastern part of the country. Then it was on to the Indonesian city of Jakarta. From there she traveled to Borobudur where she touched the sacred Buddha, an act that supposedly brought good fortune to those who could reach it. After a stop in Bangkok, her next destination was Kathmandu, Nepal. She was met at the airport and transported to her hotel, Tiger Tops, by elephant. Due to the remote nature of the hotel, the guests were shuttled on top of huge pachyderms. Tiger Tops is a famous hotel built on stilts in the jungles of Nepal. Its unique architecture allows the hotel guests to view the wild animals from a safe distance up above. From there, it was off to India, a land of stark contrasts among the social classes. She visited Calcutta, known for its abject poverty, took a boat ride on the sacred Ganges River, and saw people bathing their elephants or burning bodies upriver while others washed their clothes or bathed in it downstream. Those scenes were sharply contrasted by the serene beauty of the Taj Mahal in Agra.

Her next stop was the Middle East. Tensions after the October 1973 war made it very difficult to travel from Israel to an Arab country, so from Israel, Mary had to go to Cyprus in order to get to Beirut. She said she was always a little nervous when they'd look at her passport in that region. Her bravery served her well there and in later years. At that time, Beirut was known as the Paris of the Middle East. Unfortunately, after years of civil wars and terrorist activity, it is no longer the place of beauty Mary experienced. Details of the rest of her trip after Beirut are sketchy, but she made it home after this epic adventure. It became one of the things that fascinated me about this remarkable woman who was destined to be my wife. I didn't know it at the time because I was a struggling, long-haired flower shop co-owner in Chicago. I had a minor travel adventure of my own under my belt—a solo trip to Hawaii at eighteen years old, but that paled by comparison.

Upon her return to Iowa City, she began looking for another travel job. That's how she became affiliated with AAA. She was hired by manager Joanne as a travel agent, and when Joanne decided to leave AAA in 1978, she recommended Mary Kasper for the manager position. Mary became instant friends with all her employees, and they loved her.

Mary flourished in that position. She managed the entire travel agency and Auto Club operations. She was so well thought of by AAA Iowa headquarters that she was designated to oversee the construction of their new Towncrest office located on Muscatine Avenue. She negotiated with subcontractors, and went nose to nose with them if she felt they weren't doing their job. Her powers of charm and persuasion were legendary. She would not settle for a statement like, "We can't do that!" Any contractor who made that statement to Mary usually regretted it. In her own inimitable way, she would take that person by the arm, and say, "Let's take a little walk." By the time they'd made a circuit around the parking lot, the recalcitrant contractor was not only agreeing to what Mary was suggesting, but was doing it with the biggest smile on his face. Any of her former employees who witnessed Mary in action would wholeheartedly agree with me. She could charm the eyes out of a snake!

Mary was also very well-liked by her customers. When they returned from the exotic trips Mary set up for them, they would lavish her with gifts and kudos for her recommendations. Despite being the office manager, Mary had quite a following of former customers who would deal with no one else. She was also in great demand to escort AAA groups, particularly to Israel. She was like the proverbial mother hen, marshaling her devoted group members through the Via Dolorosa, the Temple Mount, Masada, and the many other incredible points of interest in the Holy Land. Being a great student of history and a lover of travel made Mary the most fascinating tour guide. Groups that Mary escorted were nearly always sold out. She handled group travel for Dan Gable, the legendary University of Iowa wrestling team coach, and endeared herself to those young college wrestlers. She was also pegged to lead groups when the Iowa Hawkeyes football team played in the Rose Bowl.

Most people go to AAA for road maps and vacations. I went there to find a wife...only I didn't know it at the time.

5

The Farmer's Daughter

THE LONG BUSINESS LUNCH

The travel business—particularly to Hawaii—was in a slump, so my first job in the Hawaii market ended when Roberts Hawaii Tours decided to stick with ground operations and give up its retail travel packages. As luck would have it, after a number of false starts, I was recommended to Island Holidays by a Chicago travel agent who happened to like me. I finally landed a job as a Sales Representative.

I became a Midwest Sales Rep for Island Holidays in 1979, and began to notice that a small AAA Travel Agency in Iowa City was giving me a fair number of passengers every month. I researched it and found that the office was doing an incentive program with a local mortgage company, and that accounted for the steady stream of Hawaii business. Large companies use travel and other rewards to motivate employees to be more productive. In this case, a mortgage company was using my Hawaii travel packages as rewards for top agents in eastern Iowa. I decided that it was time I drove to Iowa and met the manager to see if I could help them do more.

During my first visit, I was able to speak to the manager, Mary Kasper, for only about ten minutes because she had a conflicting commitment and could not have lunch with me. I was immediately taken with her gorgeous smile and outgoing personality. I knew I had to get to know her. I spoke to her staff and left the office. I made several attempts on subsequent visits to take her to lunch, with no luck. On my fourth visit, I spoke to the assistant manager, Agnes, and after being rejected again because of "commitments," I left without taking Mary out to lunch. Shortly after I walked out, Agnes went into Mary's office, stood in the doorway with her hands on her hips and said, "What's wrong with you; you're so rude to that boy!" Mary replied, "Oh, Agnes, I've seen them all, he's so good looking; he's either gay or married and took off his ring." (Years later when she told me this story, all I could think was, *She thought I was gay?*) Agnes replied, "He is NOT. He's single and lives at home with his mother!" To this day, I don't know how Agnes got that out of me, but the sad thing is, it was true and it probably gave Mary even more cause to be concerned.

At twenty-nine I still lived at home in Chicago with my mom and dad, and before anyone thinks it odd, I had a very good reason. Besides the fact that I had a rather tenuous travel career and had struggled in two failed businesses in my twenties, I had few assets to use to move out. But the real reason was much more painful. My baby sister, Cathy, was stricken with schizophrenia in her late teens, and my parents had no idea how to deal with her. I just could not leave home and let my folks struggle with her illness. My maternal grandmother was mentally ill and hospitalized at Chicago Reed Mental Health Center from 1938 to 1958, so my family's method of dealing with mental illness was to either ignore it or hide it away. I stayed home to help Cathy and my parents through the early years of this devastating disease. This could be the subject of another book, so I'll leave it at that.

My niece Lisa was born on Sunday, June 22, 1980, and I was scheduled to leave for Iowa the next day. I was anxious to stay in town to see my newborn niece, but I already had appointments set up for the week, including lunch with one Mary Kasper at AAA Travel Agency in Iowa City. Yes, she finally agreed to have lunch with me after Agnes's little lecture. I made it to Iowa City on Wednesday, and Ms. Kasper allowed me the honor of having lunch with her at Diamond Dave's, a nearby bar and restaurant. Mary could remember every nuance of that two-hour lunch. All I remember is that the more I talked to her, the more it felt like I had known her forever, yet I wanted to know more. We spoke very little about business and more about all of the things we had in common: we were both raised Catholic but were no longer practicing, both of us were the second of four children, we had fathers who liked to drink beer, and we were the proud aunt or uncle of at least one niece or nephew. She enthusiastically spoke of her oldest niece, Kristin Diane, and the slightly younger nephew John Dennis. Both children were the apple of their Aunt Mary's eye, and although John Dennis lived in Tomah, Wisconsin, he was just as dear to her as Kristin, who lived in Iowa City. Mary talked fondly of her Saturdays with Kristin. She had a standing date each week with the little one—who was not quite two at the time—to spend the afternoon together, either picking raspberries or doing the other things that a youngster loves to do. At thirty-two, Mary was single and had never married, so all of her love and affection was focused on those two children. I found that to be an endearing quality.

We decided that we needed to get back to work, so I drove Mary back to the Towncrest AAA office. I suppose we both knew something special had happened during that business lunch. We pulled up right in front of the office with its large window and saw her entire staff peeking out through the drapes and from behind the brochure racks. I turned to Mary and said, "I don't suppose it would be appropriate for me to kiss you." She replied, "No, I don't think so." So I took her hand and kissed it.

I sealed my fate shortly thereafter when she invited me to stay the weekend at her house. As tempted as I was, I told her that I had to get back to Chicago to see my sister's newborn daughter. She was disappointed, but that one sentence told her more about me than that entire two-hour meeting. This single, twenty-nine- year-old man, who she considered "cute as a bug's ear," was so family oriented that he would give up the opportunity to stay the weekend, just so he could see his newborn niece. Mary walked back into the travel agency. One of her employees later told me that Mary had the biggest "shit-eatin' grin on her face." According to Mary—and this is a detail I don't recall—I sent her a card that had the image of two ponies snuggling on the front cover. I think we both knew that we'd met the person we were going to marry and spend the rest of our lives with.

Mary and I would spend the weekends together when I would go out to Iowa for sales calls. At the time, Mary co-owned a house on East Washington Street with her sister Carolyn, who she called Dede (pronounced *Dee-Dee*). Dede was an elementary school teacher in Solon, so she was usually home correcting papers in the family room on the weekends, dressed in her bib overalls. On one occasion I came to the house, saw Dede doing what she always did, and remarked, "Hi, Dede, wearing your bibbies again, eh?" I didn't know it then, but Dede had a rather low opinion of this smart-ass Italian guy from Chicago who drove a Cadillac and had her sister "head over heels." Her fears that I would break Mary's heart were premature, but not that far off base.

Mary was the warmest, most passionate woman I had ever known, so our weekends in Iowa were spent in her bedroom. We would occasionally get together with her friends, but never with her family, other than her sisters. I wanted to meet her parents, but she always said, "I don't want to share you with anyone yet." I finally did meet her parents, and once I did, I instantly loved them. I'm not sure what their first impressions of me were, but when they found out I was close to my family and grew up in a close-knit Chicago neighborhood, they quickly warmed up to me. Mary was very fond of her parents, and I'm sure their opinion of her new beau was important to her. Perhaps she wanted to be sure I was "the One" before she introduced me. My mom always told me that she could tell I was hooked the moment I told her that I met "the farmer's daughter—and she has a full set of teeth!"

6

The Dating Game

SUNDAYS WITH SINATRA

I used to tease Mary that I would go to my grave hearing the story of how it took so long for me to marry her. To this day, it remains my biggest regret, especially after having lost my beloved girl after twenty years of marriage. We could have done so much more. In the first years of our relationship, we'd see each other during my sales trips to Iowa and occasionally during AAA staff trips to Chicago. During that time, unbeknownst to Mary, I was involved with a woman I met a year earlier at Echols Travel School.

Her name was Janice and she was a fascinating, sophisticated, beautiful woman with whom I had hoped to have a relationship. She and her husband were estranged but still living together in Hinsdale, Illinois, so I held back my advances. Janice just needed a sympathetic ear, so there was never any chance that she and I could be together, except as good friends. Unfortunately, I didn't know it then and wasted precious time that could have been spent with Mary. Fool that I was, I was attracted to Mary, but saw her infrequently, so at the same time I courted Janice in hopes of getting her to accompany me on a trip to Rome. I knew that Janice was fascinated with Italy, and I knew she was enamored with my Italian surname, so I thought it would be a sure thing. She was tempted to go, but kept coming up with reasons why she could not. Finally, in a last desperate attempt, I sent her a dozen red roses with a green, white, and red bow (the colors of the Italian flag), and that was enough to get her to say yes. Before you think me a cad, remember that Mary was the "other" woman; I was in love with Mary and unsure about Janice, so I had to know how this tryst was going to play out. I could probably have lied to Mary, but that was simply not an option for me because I really cared about her. I had to tell her even though there was a chance of losing her.

Mary was coming to town with her AAA staff for a mini Chicago "fam" (familiarization) trip. I met up with them one evening and asked her if we could have a private dinner together. She agreed so we went to Pizzeria Due and I gently told her that I was taking Janice to Italy. It was a very tearful experience and it makes me cringe when I think about it. I took her back to her hotel and left her there in tears. This sweet, soulful, loving woman had her heart broken by the man she loved dearly. She blamed herself and cried that she'd never be married. The scoundrel who broke her heart longed to be the one to console her, but from what I was told later, she was inconsolable. I'm not proud of what I did. But the bottom line is—and I always reminded Mary of it—I married Mary Kasper, didn't I?

The trip to Rome was both disappointing and a great relief at the same time. Janice had hardly held my hand in Italy, let alone made love with me. Early into the trip she confided that she was in love with a married man, a minor celebrity in Chicago. And she knew I was in love with Mary. Janice had no intentions of giving me a chance. During a moment of smug ego-centricity, I thought to myself, *How could she give up a chance to be with me for some cheesy lounge singer who had a wife he had no intention of leaving?* I never asked Janice why she came to Rome with me. I just politely accepted her explanation and had to beat the Italians back with a stick the entire time. Never take an attractive blond woman who wears cowgirl boots to Rome unless you want to constantly fend off the obnoxious and horny Italian men all day long.

Janice died just months before Mary at age fifty-nine from complications of lupus. She was single and probably still in love with her minor celebrity. The odd thing is that after Mary and I reunited, Mary befriended Janice and came to love her. We all remained good friends up until the day Janice died. Mary realized that Janice was not a threat, but was a sweet woman who never had designs on me and was taken advantage of by an unscrupulous lounge singer. The sad irony for me is that if things had worked out for Janice and me, and we got married, I would still be a widower today.

———

Mary escorted a trip to Scandinavia for AAA Travel that fall. As manager, part of her job was to fill the trip so she could qualify for the free, tour conductor pass allowed by the airline. Mary was very charming and persuasive, so she proceeded to recruit all of her "old maid" friends (her words) and signed them all up for the two-week trip visiting Norway, Copenhagen, and Sweden. The approximate $1,300 cost included airfare, hotels, two meals a day, sightseeing, and the services of Mary Kasper, tour director extraordinaire. She needed only one more person to qualify for the tour conductor pass, so she asked her sister Carolyn to go along. Carolyn declined because she thought it was too expensive and she didn't have that kind of money just lying around. Mary said to her, "C'mon Dede, take a loan out against a CD and come with us." Carolyn balked but finally gave in and took out a loan against a certificate of deposit. The ladies —Judy, Becky, Sandy, Linda Marie, Carolyn, and Mary—all went on the trip, and something strange happened. Linda Marie was chronically late for each departing bus because she stayed up late reading in a dry bathtub (so she could have the light on and not disturb Mary). But more interesting than that, Carolyn fell madly in love with the bus driver two days into the trip. Bjorn was six years younger than she. They were inseparable, and when it came time to fly home, Dede cried all the way across the North Atlantic. "Why did I have to meet and fall in love with a man who lives half way around the world?" she wailed. "I'll never see him again." With that, she promptly tore up his phone number.

A few days after they returned to Iowa City, the phone rang; it was Bjorn crying on the phone that he loved her and wanted to marry her. He announced that he was coming to Iowa and arrived about a month later. He stayed a month and they decided that Carolyn would go to Norway at

Christmas. When she came back she announced that they were going to get married in the spring and move to Norway. Carolyn did not see Bjorn again until he arrived for the wedding with his mother, father, uncle, and aunts. The only one in the group who spoke English was Bjorn. They were married in an English-Norwegian ceremony at the Zion Lutheran Church in Iowa City. For their honeymoon all seven of them rented a Winnebago and went to Yellowstone National Park! I imagine it was quite interesting going on a honeymoon in a small motor home with five in-laws who do not speak English! Naturally, Mary's parents blamed her for not breaking up this alliance, because they didn't want their Carolyn moving to Norway. But in the end, they grew to love Bjorn, and how happy he made their eldest daughter.

Remember, I had not been invited to the wedding because I took someone else to Rome, so I heard all about this much later when we were back together. Months had gone by with no communication between Mary and me. I wrote Mary a letter apologizing to her for not calling, blaming my uncle's recent passing and other convenient excuses. Being the dunce that I was, I told her that I missed her and put a PS at the end of the letter saying, "Rome was wonderful." I meant that Rome—the city—was wonderful. Mary's interpretation of that sentence was that Rome and my wild passionate fling with Janice were wonderful.

When Mary finally agreed to speak to me, I explained to her that nothing happened with Janice. I thanked her for letting me figure out that she (Mary) was the one I loved. I loved her for believing me and I loved her for giving me another chance. I know I broke her heart, but she forgave me and turned out to be the best thing that ever happened to me.

From that point on, we renewed our love affair and spent some of the most memorable times together. As a travel agency manager, back in the days when there were perks in that outrageously low-paying business, Mary would get free passes on Mississippi Valley Airlines, which was fondly known as "Mud Valley Airlines" in the trade. They flew those boxy, Irish-built airplanes called the Shorts 30. They were loud, unpressurized turbo prop planes that made the short hops between Cedar Rapids and Chicago's O'Hare Airport back in the eighties.

In the early eighties, I moved out of my parents' house and into the apartment in the building my brother and I owned in Chicago. It was in a late 20's era building that housed the flower shop we ran until 1977. We never made any money in the flower business, but we were able to buy the building with my dad's financial help. I lived in the 1,600-square-foot, two-bedroom apartment on the second floor. It had a formal dining room and a huge living room. There were hardwood floors throughout, and a natural fireplace that my brother, my dad, and I installed.

Mary would fly up to Chicago and spend the weekends with me. We were like bunnies back then, and couldn't get enough of each other. Some days we would stay in bed and make love all day. Oh, what stamina we had!

One of our favorite things to do was on Sunday evenings. We would roll up the big area rug in the living room, light a fire in the winter, and listen to Norman Mark's radio show entitled *Sundays with Sinatra*. We would dance for hours to Frank's ballads, stopping only to make love when the passion became overwhelming. Mary was a passionate and wonderful dancer. She did not like to dance fast, but she was the most fabulous slow dancer who followed my every turn. She always told me how much she loved to dance with me, but I think it was the other way around. I was taught to dance by my mother at Polish weddings. She would take me out on the dance floor, and that's how I learned to cut a rug, but Mary was just a natural.

We would have to stop dancing around 10 p.m. to race to O'Hare so she could catch the last flight out on MVA. More often than not, because she was flying Space A (space available) she'd get bumped off the flight. Then it was a mad dash downtown to the sleazy Greyhound bus terminal to catch the midnight bus to Iowa City. Mary always laughed about "doggin' it" home. She loved me so much that she'd spend five hours overnight riding to Iowa with her purse tucked under her head and some unsavory people sitting around her. She'd bunch up her sweater to use as a pillow and sleep the entire way home. She'd get in around 5a.m. or so, grab a cab to her house, shower, eat some breakfast, and be at work by 7:30 a.m. We played out that scenario over and over again. I used to tell Mary that she was GUD (Geographically Undesirable) because she lived three and a half hours away. In the early days, neither one of us considered moving because we both had good jobs that would not allow us to live in each other's town. Again, if I had any brains, I would have figured out how to marry her right away. It hurts me to think of how much more time we could have had as man and wife.

7

Brassieres on the Clothesline

MARY MAKES HER MOVE

At one time or another, you have to make a decision and move on it. My dad had a favorite, crudely colorful expression for indecisive people…"Shit or get off the pot." That was a Southside Chicago, blue-collar way of telling someone to hurry up. On one of Mary's winter weekend visits, when Chicago had record wind chill temperatures around -60F, I proposed. We were in my living room where the 1929-era radiators could only get the room up to a balmy 62 degrees. I did not have a ring because this was not premeditated, but I did get down on my knee to ask her to be my bride. I was so in love with her, and after our many lovemaking marathons, I realized that I could satisfy such a passionate woman. It was time to pop the question. She enthusiastically said yes and we were like giddy little children as we raced to O'Hare to catch the last flight. Luckily, she made that one. Shortly after I pledged my troth, Island Holidays laid me off. Naturally, the practical John thought, *"How am I going to support a wife?"*, so I called Mary and asked that we postpone our wedding plans. Luckily, I landed a position with Pleasant Hawaiian Holidays a few weeks later, but for some reason, I never picked up the marriage ball and ran with it. I guess cold feet have a habit of not defrosting very fast.

Mary patiently waited for me to get my act together and once again talk about marriage, but it didn't happen. I even went so far as to joke when the word came up saying with a stutter, "mum-mum-mum-marriage." I thought it was funny, but a certain someone did not see the humor in it. This went on until early 1984 when Mary decided that she needed to make a change in her lifestyle and that I needed to be a part of it. She wanted some sort of commitment from me, and if I wasn't going to make the first move, she would. Her friend and former neighbor Judy had moved to Minneapolis a few years prior to be near the man she loved. Judy and I always had somewhat of a distant relationship, probably because I broke Mary's heart once and now that we were a happy couple again, I think she was unsure of my intentions. When Mary pressured me to make a commitment, her tactic was to threaten to move elsewhere. When she said, "If you don't make up your mind, I'm going to Minneapolis and move in with Judy!" Well, that's all I had to hear. I said, "Why don't you move to Chicago and live with me for a while?" Why I didn't just say let's get married, I'll never know.

———

Mary rented out her house on Washington Street and moved to Chicago on Mother's Day 1984. She took a job downtown as City Manager for Thomas Cook Travel. By doing so, she effectively doubled her salary and was able to work in the Loop, something she found very exciting despite the forty-five-minute bus ride on the CTA (Chicago Transit Authority). I was promoted to Regional Sales Manager for Pleasant Hawaiian Holidays, so I needed to find an office space in Chicago. The storefront in my building was vacant at the time, so I approached Pleasant about renting the space from my brother and me for our Midwest Regional Sales Office. I gave them a break on the rent and they remodeled the space to make it workable. My commute consisted of a one-minute walk down the stairs as opposed to Mary's bus ride.

There were many times when I would make dinner and have it waiting for Mary when she arrived home. Sometimes I was wearing a tuxedo and had candles lit, and sometimes I was wearing only a bow tie! We laughed like little kids when we'd do fun things like that. Mary was so full of life, so ready for adventure, so positive and fun-loving that she made it fun for me to do those things for her. She teased me once that it was very cold in downtown Chicago and that most women wore fur coats. I was so in love with her that I bought her a full-length Blackglama ranch mink that she wore to work every day. The farmer's daughter wore a mink coat and tennis shoes to an office in the Equitable Building on Michigan Avenue. She was in the big leagues, and she loved it.

We spent many happy hours in that apartment, fixing it up and being a couple. My brother-in-law's mother knew that something was going on when she saw the brassieres hanging from the clothesline off the back porch. She decided that either I had a new live-in or I was experimenting with cross-dressing! We lived across the street from Miami Bowl, the world's largest (at that time) bowling alley with eighty lanes. They had a busy parking lot, and it was always fun to sit and watch the cars being stolen every night. It got to the point where we were tired of calling the police whenever we'd see someone breaking into one. Luckily, our cars were never touched.

8

A Thousand Camels For Your Wife

TRAVELS WITH MARY

Mary and I went to New Zealand in 1983. She and I had incurable wanderlust, and when she asked me where in the world I'd like to go, I immediately said New Zealand. She looked at me with the most flabbergasted look on her face and said, "That's exactly where I want to go!" Mary was so selfless that she would probably have said that to me even if she wanted to go to South America. It seemed like her life's work was to make *me* happy. I always knew we had something special—we thought alike, we liked the same things, and we were always ready for a new adventure. We had fun planning the trip and were excited about going that far together.

It started out as a memorable trip because we were in the air flying from Honolulu to Auckland when the Russians shot down Korean Airlines Flight 007. It was, and still is, a controversial incident. How does a filled-to-capacity, commercial 747 with the latest computer-guided navigation systems, and two experienced pilots, stray into Soviet airspace and get mistaken for a spy plane? Even experienced flyers get nervous when something so senseless happens while you're abroad.

Our Continental DC-10 touched down in Auckland without incident, but we were in for a surprise when the cabin crew came down both aisles spraying this foul insect fogger. It seemed that arriving international flights could be carrying agricultural pests that had to be eradicated, even if the passengers wouldn't be able to breathe. I hope the practice is no longer necessary, for the sake of all New Zealand-bound American lungs.

Auckland was nice, but the real attractions in New Zealand were out in the country. We had the pleasure of visiting Tudor Towers in Rotorua, and experiencing the melodious voices of the Maori, and their fascinating poi ball dancing. Mary was very photogenic and never failed me when I needed a willing subject. The Maori have a habit of sticking their tongues out while dancing; it was a threatening pose used to intimidate adversaries. There happened to be a Maori tiki on the premises, so Mary posed alongside it, demonstrating her version of the threatening tongue wag. It's one of my favorite pictures and a terrific example of the fun-loving nature of my girl.

Tudor Towers was a tourist attraction that showcased the English influence in New Zealand. One of their biggest draws, outside of the Maori experience, was lawn bowling. Men dressed in white, cotton cable-knit sweaters and funny-looking hats, played the genteel game on the finely manicured lawns in front of the building.

We also visited the Devil's Kitchen on the North Island. It is an area of volcanic activity that has bubbling mud pots, geysers, and steaming ponds. Once again, Mary was no shrinking violet, so she stuck her head in the cutout of the little female devil for a photo op.

When it came time to visit the South Island, we decided to fly rather than take a car ferry, so we booked passage on Mount Cook Airlines. At that time they flew small Cessna aircraft with room for only a few passengers and one pilot. Weights and balances are important in such a small airplane, so each passenger had to divulge his or her weight. We were still dating at the time, so Mary wasn't crazy about me knowing how much she weighed. All of the preflight preparations were done right on the tarmac, so Mary took the pilot for a little walk to tell him her deep, dark secret. I could see the pilot laughing as she whispered in his ear how she was concerned about safety, but also didn't want her boyfriend to know exactly how much she weighed. She walked back with him, arm in arm, smiling broadly and sticking her tongue out at me as he continued to chuckle.

She never thought she had a sense of humor, but she could have a stranger laughing at the drop of a hat. To give you an example of how different we were in our approach to things, during the flight, Mary was like an excited child looking out the window and pointing to objects below, while I sat there thinking of how I'd have to be talked down by the tower when the pilot has his heart attack! Mary teased me unmercifully about how I always had to think ahead. It is a trait I inherited from my father; he had a habit of worrying about things or "sweating the small stuff." I consider it being prepared like a Boy Scout, but she saw it as paranoia. If we were invited to go out to dinner in downtown Chicago, Mary's take on it would be, "Oh, how exciting to have dinner downtown!" and I'd say something like, "What if we can't find a parking space?" She was right; I'm just a worry wart! For Mary, the glass was always half full, and that attitude did not change even when she was diagnosed with non-Hodgkin's lymphoma years later. If anything, it made her appreciate every waking moment even more.

I like to describe New Zealand as the country in which Mother Nature took all the beautiful things in the world and put them in one place. It has beautiful tropical beaches, rain forests, volcanic activity, spectacular mountains, gorgeous pastureland, exotic wildlife, fjords to rival Norway, glowworm grottos, and charming European-style villages. It also boasts some pretty spectacular glaciers, notably the Franz Josef glacier on Mount Cook. We had a little Mitsubishi rental car that carried us all over the South Island. It also took us up to the Hermitage, a historic hotel at the top of Mount Cook near the famous glacier. Unfortunately, Mount Cook was socked in with fog, so we spent a couple of days lounging around the lobby, but that was only when we weren't in the room making love (we did a lot of that in those days).

On one particular day, when we tired of being between the sheets, we decided to sit in the lobby and plan the rest of the trip. Mary needed a map from the car, so I gave her the keys and patiently waited for her to return. It took her what seemed like an eternity to come back, so when she finally returned with a sheepish look on her face, and no map, my suspicions were confirmed. "You locked the keys in the car, didn't you?" I asked. She nearly started crying as she admitted to the deed. She had not yet learned that I didn't get upset about such things; at least I didn't back then. I quietly put down my book and took her by the hand in search of a coat hanger. Luckily, the door was ajar, so it was easy to get it open. She was always amazed at my ability to get her out of trouble. I did so on a number of occasions, and it always gave me a great feeling of being needed. Mary said my mother gave her advice when we got married. It was something to the effect of, "You won't have to carry a purse, money, or your keys because you have him now." Let me tell you, she took her at her word.

One of the things we thoroughly enjoyed during our visit to the South Island was our tour of a working sheep station. Sheep stations are vast operations usually located in remote areas, where sheep are raised primarily for wool. Very skilled young men using high-powered electric wool clippers shear the sheep periodically, and they routinely demonstrate this art for some very wide-eyed tourists. During festivals, sheep shearing competitions are always a major draw.

Part of our tour was a demonstration of the herding abilities of the dogs. A group of us went down to the pasture where the shepherd gave the dog commands by whistling. One type of whistle made the dog take two sheep from one pen and herd them over to another, while a different whistle prompted him do something else. It was impressive. When the dog finished, the shepherd called him over to us and allowed us to pet him. People asked all sorts of questions about the dog, such as, "What's his name? What does he like to eat?" All this time my Mary was looking at the sheep with her hand on her chin, then said, "Do you have a problem with hoof rot?" Everyone, including me, looked at her bewilderedly. I started to laugh thinking it was a joke, but she was dead serious! For all her world travels, fancy clothes, big house, and all the other trappings of life, Mary was a farmer's daughter who loved being on the farm in Iowa, and it showed in the most unexpected places.

———

During one of our many RV trips, we happened to be in McMinnville, Oregon, for the Linn County Fair. As was customary at county fairs, there was always animal judging going on. As we wandered through, Mary caught sight of the hog barn and decided that it would be an interesting place to watch the contest judging. Being a city boy, I was less than enthused with the idea, but because I loved her so much, I gave in. With my handkerchief deftly held over my mouth and nose, I stood there and watched at the rail with my girl as the kids proudly paraded their 4-H Club projects around the ring. There were hogs—I call them pigs—of every size, shape, and color being primped and preened, then led around the ring with a lead and a stick. I stood there breathing through my handkerchief as Mary studied each porker as it passed by her. Out of the blue she proclaimed, "That one! That's the winner! That "gilt" is the winner!". She spoke with great certainty and enthusiasm, but I just said, "Yeah, right!" thinking she was pulling my leg. I quickly mumbled through my handkerchief, "Huh, how do you know?" I just thought he had a pretty neat stripe around his body, but she saw something I didn't. She responded, "See how long and lean he is? That's what they look for in a gilt." I'll be damned if that judge didn't walk over to that very pig and place the blue ribbon on him. Mary turned to me with the biggest grin on her face as she slapped my shoulder with her hand. Then she gave me a big hug around the neck. "See, I told you so!" she exclaimed. I should have known better than to question a girl whose father raised hogs and took them to market in Chicago.

Early on in our relationship I marveled at Mary's stories about her travels around the world and her life on a farm. Sometimes the two were intermingled. One day we were cruising down Interstate 80 to or from Iowa, and she was relating a story to me about how she was detained in Syria because she had an Israeli visa in her passport. She suddenly exclaimed, "Wow, that's a nice John Deere," as she looked at the big tractor plowing the field along the interstate. My response was something like, "How in God's name do you know that it's a John Deere?" She said, "That's easy; it's green. Deeres are green, Fords are blue, and International Harvesters are red." Good God, this girl knew her tractors by their color. Who could ask for anything more?

———

Our trip to Egypt in 1984 was memorable. Mary was managing the Thomas Cook Business Travel Center in Chicago, so she was always being showered with travel perks. In those days, a high-producing travel agency manager was always being wined and dined by the airlines and travel companies. Mary managed to arrange a pretty comprehensive trip to Egypt for not a lot of money through Thomas Cook's local operation in Cairo. We flew nonstop for eleven hours from New York to Cairo on TWA. I was traveling on a reduced-fare coach ticket and Mary was being treated to complimentary first class because of her relationship with TWA. Not wanting to spend eleven hours sitting up front by herself with me in the back, she gave up her seat to the woman sitting next to me. Needless to say, the woman was very pleased to fly first class to Cairo.

We arrived in Cairo after eleven exhausting hours and disembarked onto the tarmac surrounded by armed soldiers carrying machine guns. It was a sobering first introduction to the Third World for me. We entered the aged and dingy airport terminal and saw our names on a placard held up by an unkempt young Egyptian man named Hagag. Hagag escorted us to our waiting transportation, which was a well-worn Mercedes being dusted off by an older Egyptian man.

The ride into Cairo was harrowing, to say the least. Mary remarked that my eyes were as wide as saucers as the driver sped into the city. Drivers had a unique way of approaching an intersection in Cairo...instead of paying attention to cross traffic, Egyptian drivers simply leaned on their horns as they sped through. I'd never again criticize Chicago cab drivers after that experience.

The poverty in Cairo was overwhelming. The air was full of pollution. People were actually living on the center medians of the highway and city buses that were designed for fifty people had another dozen or so hanging on the sides and rear. The Muslim call to prayer was ever present and gave an eerie quality to the scenery.

We were booked into the Cairo Marriott Hotel on an island in the Nile River. It was a luxurious respite from Cairo. We visited many sites in Egypt, including the Aswan High Dam, built by the Soviets during the term of Nasser; Abu Simbel, the ancient temple to Ramses that was taken apart and moved in 1966 when the new dam threatened to put it underwater; Luxor, the Valley of the Kings; the Karnac and Luxor temples; and the temple to queen Hatshepsut, the only female pharaoh in Ancient Egypt. Our guide Hagag gave us a great way to remember her name: he motioned as if he were tipping his hat and pointed out his cheap suit.

A highlight of the trip had to be our entry into the tomb of Tutankhamen. We descended the stairs into the dimly lit burial chamber and marveled at the elaborate murals that graced the walls. It was exciting to pretend that it was the 1920s and we were with Harold Carter as he discovered this first complete tomb of an Egyptian pharaoh. I think the Tut curse is alive and well because just as I was looking over the sarcophagus, my bowels began to rumble, and later that day, I was the victim of food poisoning. I had diarrhea for two days and suffered the indignity of having to use the public facilities in Egypt. You entered a public restroom to find there was no toilet paper because a Bedouin had collected the rolls and was selling it by the sheet at the door. The airport restrooms were foul, to say the least, so I could not wait to board the flight to Cairo in a brand new Egypt Air 767 with its nice, clean restrooms.

Part of the tour was a trip to the pyramids. Naturally, there was an Egyptian there with a camel, offering rides for $5. We had heard stories of camel rides that cost $5, and then you found out that it was $25 to bring you back, so we decided on a photo op only. That's when the camel driver offered me, "A thousand camels for your wife!" Mary was flattered by the offer and I saw it as a cheesy way to stroke the tourists. The worst part of all that was when he took off my baseball cap and put it on his head. I don't think the man had washed his hair recently, so I let him keep it. He came very close to placing his headpiece on me, but I ducked in the nick of time.

The best part of our trip to Egypt was when Hagag bribed a guard and got us into one of the Great Pyramids—the middle one known as Khafre. We walked into the narrow passageway and climbed down to the burial chamber in the very center. We looked around in awe at the graffiti left behind in the nineteenth century, and marveled at the silence as the two of us stood there looking up and around the interior. When it came time to leave, we started up the narrow shaft toward the light. As soon as Mary stepped in front of me her body blocked the light at the entrance to the tunnel. I immediately remarked, "Who turned out the lights?" a veiled reference to the size of her butt. She couldn't turn around in the tunnel, so she started laughing and threatened me with bodily harm. We came out of that tunnel into the sunshine and giggled like children over what we had just seen, and gave each other a big, sloppy kiss. That's how Mary and I approached everything…with laughter and deep affection for each other.

9

Ooh la la

AN AMERICAN IN PARIS

After moving in with me, Mary rekindled her love affair with cooking. Now that she had someone to cook for, she regularly experimented on me. I enjoyed most of her creations, save for one...Welsh rarebit. I cringe every time I think about that glob of foul cheese on toast!

One day Mary arrived home from work and was just bubbling with excitement. She was jumping up and down and said, "We're going to Paris!" Knowing that she was always getting free tickets to Europe, I was puzzled by her excitement. "Okay, sure, when do you want to go, and why?" I asked because she seemed to have a purpose. "I want a set of copper pots, and my friend Karen told me where to get them in Paris. She goes every few months and brings home a couple of each in her carry-on, so she doesn't have to ship and wait for months." Karen was a sales rep for United Airlines, so she too had a pocket full of free tickets back then. I agreed because I would never pass up a chance to go to Paris. Let's just say that I rarely said no to Mary. I was so in love, I just wanted to shower her with gifts, and if she wanted to go to Paris to buy copper pots, then we would go to Paris and do just that! I used to laugh and recite this little rhyme: What Mary wants, Mary gets. What Johnny wants, he forgets! Boy, did that get her dander up!

On our first copper pot adventure, we flew to Paris and visited Versailles, took a boat ride on the Bateaux Mouches Seine river cruise, and toured Notre Dame Cathedral. We took the Paris metro to the Georges Pompidou Centre stop and walked the short distance to 18 rue Coquilliere, the home of E. Dehillerin, a family-owned shop founded in 1820 that provides *materiel de cuisine* for gourmet and hobby chefs alike. Mary was like a kid in a candy store. This wondrous kitchen store was packed with every culinary utensil you could possibly imagine, and in every conceivable size. I have never seen so many wire whisks in my life, from the very tiny to the gigantic, and one so large it would take two hands to use it. And copper cookware was everywhere...hanging from the ceiling, wrapped in brown paper, and stacked on shelves all the way to the ceiling. Sawdust was on the floor, and disinterested salespeople were everywhere...this was Paris, after all. As I said in a previous chapter, Mary could charm the eyes out of a snake, so it did not take long for her to endear herself to a handsome young salesclerk. We purchased two pieces that day, one for each carry-on. We completed the set on subsequent trips and became the only household in our neighborhood to have authentic copper pots from Paris.

One trip was especially memorable because it was a classic example of Mary's positive effect on people, even Parisians. We walked into Dehillerin that day and Mary quickly recognized the young man who waited on us the time before. She thought he was very handsome, and therefore hard to forget. She went right up to him and said, "Hello, young man, will you help us?" He raised an eyebrow and said with a classic Maurice Chevalier accent, "How did you know I speak English, mademoiselle?" Mary replied as he grasped her hand, "Oh, you helped us buy some copper pots last year." He raised her hand to his lips, kissed it tenderly, then said, "I never forget a beautiful woman...what is your name?" She blushed as she replied, "Mary DiViggiano." Still holding her hand, he remarked, "DiViggiano...*Oh là là. Italiano...c'est magnifique.*" She worked her magic and had that young man eating out of her hand. We purchased a couple more pieces for the collection and came away from that encounter with a new story to tell about yet another adventure.

Mary decided that she needed a small double boiler for melting chocolate, so we made another trip to Paris and back to Dehillerin. Mary's young man wasn't there that day, but we had no trouble finding what she was looking for. But I know she was disappointed.

On this visit to Paris, we went to see two of the more macabre Paris attractions, Père Lachaise Cemetery and the Parisian catacombs; the former being the burial place of Chopin and Oscar Wilde, amongst others, and, of course, Jim Morrison of the Doors. Youngsters who weren't even born when he was popular surrounded his grave. They were all sitting around smoking marijuana, lighting candles, and seemingly holding a vigil until he rose from the dead! It is a bizarre scene.

The catacombs are an eerie series of Roman tunnels that stretch for miles under the city. They house the bones of millions of dead from the cemeteries of Paris that were emptied out as the city grew. The bones are neatly piled in niches throughout the tunnels, with skulls to adorn the front of the stacks. There are plaques stating the name of the cemetery and the year it was closed. And there is a Latin greeting above the archway to the first chamber that translates to: You Are Entering the Realm of the Dead. It is cool, dark, and creepy…and we loved it! You must climb a spiral staircase to exit the catacombs and are greeted at the top by a guard sitting at a small table. The table had a small pile of bones and a child's skull sitting on top. At that point, everyone is subject to having purses and bags searched…yes, people steal the bones!

On one of our early trips to Paris in the 1980s, we met a charming South African couple while sipping coffee al fresco at the famous Café De La Paix, across the street from the Paris Opera House. Obie and Suzanne were on holiday in Paris, and happened to sit next to us at a sidewalk table. Mary was not one to ignore interesting people who happen to be sitting shoulder to shoulder with us, so she struck up a conversation with them. Obie was a pilot of some ilk, and Suzanne a homemaker, who happened to speak fluent French. Needless to say, because of Mary's magnetic personality (I'm no slouch, but I pale by comparison), we became fast friends and toured Paris with them over the next two days.

It was Obie who shot my favorite picture of Mary and me, sitting on a park bench, kissing with the Eiffel Tower looming in the background. My heart leaps every time I see that photograph, and it's not because I'm wearing a Members Only jacket. We were two thirty-something Americans, and we were crazy about each other. There we were, two people so much in love, kissing in the shadow of the symbol of Paris, the most romantic city in the world. It was a magic moment—one of more than I can count. Being in love, and being loved, is the most magical experience in any setting. But in Paris, every single display of love or affection seems deeper, truer, and more meaningful. Paris is called the City of Light. To us, it was always the City of Love.

10

A Concert With Vows

JOHN AND MARY WED

Mary lived with me in Chicago for nearly two years and made me so happy I felt it was time we made our arrangement permanent. We happened to be shopping at a local mall in the fall of 1985 when Mary wandered into a jewelry store (she had a habit of doing that). She began looking at emerald and diamond rings and had the clerk bring one out that caught her eye. It was just shy of $2,000. She put the ring on her finger and promptly fell in love with it. It was a .75 ct emerald-cut emerald, nearly perfect, with two small brilliant-cut diamonds on either side. As Mary admired it, I asked her a question, "Is that your idea of an engagement ring?" She responded, "Ohhhh, yes!" I looked up at the clerk and said, "We'll take it." Mary spun around with her hand still in the air and said, "What do you mean, we'll take it?" Without allowing me to answer, she handed the ring back to the clerk and told her, "We'll be right back." She grabbed me by the hand and dragged me out into the mall, then said, "What's this all about?" I responded by saying, "I love you and I think we should get married…don't you agree?" She flashed her world-famous smile and simply said, "Yes, yes, yes!" as she jumped into my arms and kissed me passionately. We walked back into the store with huge grins on our faces and purchased the ring.

On the ride home we talked about a date and I mentioned that perhaps a year later, in September of '86 would be nice. Her response was, "Oh, really? Well, I think we should get married in May!" I'm sure the nature of her response was directly related to the false starts we had earlier in our engagement.

I don't blame Mary for wanting to forge ahead and set a date. I guess I just thought we'd need at least a year to make plans. Not so. Not when Mary Kasper is doing the planning! Once again, this clearly defined the differences between us. I'm the careful planner, always thinking ahead about contingencies, and Mary was the get 'er done, take charge, make it happen type. And that was always one of her most remarkable qualities. I'm that way too, but only once I've begun the project and have come out of the planning stages. Mary was always amazed how I would take on a project and not rest until it was completed. She'd always say, "Boy, when you put your mind to something, you get it done!" She probably didn't know it, but much of that was rubbed off from her.

The date would be May 17, 1986, and the place would be Zion Lutheran Church in Iowa City, Iowa. We were both raised Catholic but had stopped practicing many years earlier. My decision was made after spending twelve years in parochial schools and having had my share of Dominican nuns and Christian Brothers. Let's just say that much of their time was wasted. Not that I'm an atheist...I'd prefer to think of myself as agnostic, someone who wants to believe but is struggling with the concept. At the time, Mary's sister Jane was married to a Lutheran minister who happened to be the assistant pastor at a church in Mason City, so we decided that he should perform the ceremony. After all, he was family.

After months of planning, we drove out to Iowa a few days prior and spent the time at Joe's and Mel's house. They felt it was okay for us to sleep in the same bedroom because it had twin beds...the most uncomfortable beds in the universe. There was always something so forbidden about making love in those twin beds with her folks in the next room. There we'd be, like a couple of naughty kids rolling around under the covers, shushing each other as we did what came so naturally back then.

May 17, 1986 dawned with overcast skies and the threat of heavy rain. Oh, well, there was no stopping us now. Being the Virgo that I am, I simply could not stand the thought of my car being dirty at my wedding, so I dragged out the hose on Joe's driveway and started washing my 1984 Cadillac Eldorado in the drizzle.

At the time, it was my dream car, black on black with black leather interior. Black, was the undisputed "power color." Every successful person drove a black car, or so I thought. To me, a black Cadillac meant you'd arrived. Your ship had come in. You've made it. I have had eight Cadillacs in my life so far, and with the exception of two, all were black. One of the two odd-colored ones was in Joe's garage. I sold Joe my 1983 Sedan Deville, because the salesman told me that it was the hottest color in 1983, but neglected to tell me that every other GM car sold that year had it too. It was that rose-beige paint job with a brown vinyl top. I saw myself coming and going everywhere I looked...every Chevy, Buick, and Oldsmobile offered that color combination so it was omnipresent. I could only stomach that for a year, so I sold the Caddy to Joe and Mel and bought a brand new black Eldorado. I believe that's when the "No Nail Polish" rule was laid down, warning of dire consequences! Every "piffle" comment was met with a scowl that could curdle your blood, but not Mary's. She could be so defiant. She often told me the story of how, as a little girl, she defied her dad's request by refusing to get up out of her chair to do something. Joe reached down to pick her up and she clamped her hands down on the arms of that chair so tight, the chair came with her. Mary inherited her defiance and her short temper from Joe. He was a pretty headstrong guy, so you wanted to stay on his good side, but he had a heart of gold and loved his girls...and he loved anyone who loved his girls too.

As I worked on the car that morning, I moved around to the front to rinse off the soap, and the hose proceeded to catch on the front tire. I gave it a yank to free it, and it freed up much too easily. My left hand flung itself right into the brick wall of the garage, tearing flesh off my left ring finger's knuckle. I came inside holding my bloody hand. I can still see the horrified look on Mary's face. We cleaned it up and found that it wasn't as serious as it looked, but it did make for a difficult ring ceremony later that day.

My mother, Helen, kept saying that it was good luck to have rain on your wedding day. Well, let's just say we had buckets of good luck that day. It rained, and rained, and rained, and rained until it couldn't rain anymore. The only time it stopped raining was right after the ceremony, so we at least had a chance to get into our cars—our clean cars that is—without getting soaked.

Mary loved classical music and we were fortunate that Zion Lutheran was very musically inclined. My brother-in-law, the minister, was also a talented carpenter who had a hand in rebuilding the church's pipe organ, so we made use of that. His mother was one of the bell ringers for the church, so she and her group played Pachelbel's Canon on the hand bells. We had a violinist, an organist, and the bells. The processional and recessional were Bach, with interludes of Brahms and others. That prompted our friend Rebecca to say, "It was like a concert with vows."

We decided that since we weren't kids, we'd walk down the aisle together. As we stood at the back of the church waiting, Mary looked at me and asked, "Are you nervous?" I replied, "No, you're only nervous if you're not sure."

Our two nephews, John Dennis and Nicholas—ages seven and four, respectively—were the ring bearers dressed in blue blazers and khaki pants. Our nieces, Kristin and Lisa—ages eight and six—were the flower girls and had pink, frilly dresses. They were all adorable, and each one made the ceremony very entertaining for the congregation. John was fascinated by the big chandeliers overhead, so he kept craning his neck to look up above, and Nick liked to make faces at his sister who was facing him across the altar. He raised his eyebrows up and down and whispered to his sister, "Kristin, Kristin, we get to keep the piddows!" He then turned to tell John Dennis and suddenly his father's big hand came down on his little head and cranked it back to the front. Little Kristin lost a flower out of her bouquet and was determined to get it. She tried desperately to slowly kneel down on one knee and carefully pick it up without falling over. She succeeded, and every eye in the church was upon her. Lisa just stood there with her little hands folded in prayer as her favorite aunt and uncle said their vows. Mary's sister Jane was her matron of honor, and my brother Tony was best man. As we walked down the aisle as husband and wife, everyone remarked that we both had wide grins on our faces. Another friend commented, "It was so refreshing to see two adults getting married."

After formal pictures were taken in the church, we drove about thirty miles east to the town of Tipton, Iowa, where we had a reception for about ninety guests at the Victorian House of Tipton, a beautifully restored nineteenth-century mansion. We had drinks and a lavish buffet as the rain poured down outside. During the evening, we received a call from our tenants in the Iowa City house telling us that water was coming in under the basement door...mind you, on our wedding day. My response was, "Buy a shop vac, suck it up, and send me the bill!" We spent the night in the gorgeous main bedroom of the mansion. After saying goodnight to the last guest, we dragged ourselves upstairs, and discovered a bed full of rice. Mary's aunt Mag and my cousin Pat did the dirty deed. There we were, scooping rice into champagne glasses before hopping into the big four-poster "rice" bed (a classic bed style with sheaves of rice carved on the posts). We both had too much champagne and could have easily gone to sleep, but I said, "I'll be damned if I don't make love to my new wife on my wedding night!" So we consummated our marriage as we continued to pick errant grains of rice out of the bed.

In the morning, the sun shone brightly on the soggy landscape, and Mary discovered that she had forgotten to bring a change of clothes. So she rode back dressed in my T-shirt, gym shorts, and leather jacket instead of her wedding dress. That was the first clue as to how interesting and fun our marriage was to be.

11

How Much You Pay?

HONEYMOON IN CHINA

Where do two world travelers spend their honeymoon in the year 1986? Why, in Mainland China, where else? Yes, John and Mary were not about to settle for someplace as mundane as Acapulco or Niagara Falls, we opted for a three-week adventure in China, which was newly opened to tourism from the West. We had free air tickets and a deeply discounted package tour through American Express, so off we went that following June to the People's Republic of China. After a brief stopover in Hawaii, we flew nonstop to Hong Kong to begin our Chinese adventure. Flying into Kai-Tak Airport is always a thrill, one that a nervous flyer would probably want to do with closed eyes. You literally come in for a landing between apartment buildings, and you'd swear the wing tips are going to run afoul of the laundry hanging from clotheslines. The few days we spent in Hong Kong were exciting and fun. Mary had been there several times, so she enjoyed showing me the sights. We had high tea at the Peninsula Hotel, which has a fleet of Rolls-Royces to shuttle its guests around town, and shopped at Stanley Market, the most famous flea market in the world. Mary insisted that I had some shirts custom made while in Hong Kong, so she took me to a tailor in the promenade of the Excelsior Hotel. I was fitted for four dress shirts, complete with monograms, and in a few days they were ready to be picked up at only $12 each. I have never since had shirts that fit me so well.

After meeting our group in Hong Kong, we were off to Mainland China for the most memorable adventure Mary and I have ever had. We came away with a new phrase about a visit to China in 1986: there are two things you don't want to miss on your trip to China...the Great Wall and your flight home! China's infrastructure was not ready for Westerners so the facilities were somewhat lacking. We stayed in only one new Western hotel, the Garden Hotel in Guangzhou (Canton). It was a brand-new Swiss-owned hotel with all the modern comforts we were accustomed to. Even so, we had to drink bottled water and sleep in twin beds. In 1986 the Chinese had a long way to go with regards to Western-style customer service. Our wet bath towels would be folded and neatly put on the shelves, so most of the time we had to steal fresh towels off the maid's cart in the hallway. Outside of the hotels, the public facilities left much to be desired. Restrooms were generally not Western-style, in that they amounted to a hole in the floor with footprints on either side. In many cases, there was no running water in the restroom and mosquitoes would come streaming out when you relieved yourself. Mary was a real sport about it and just chalked it up to being in the Third World. I had to enter with my handkerchief over my face! This was the time before hand sanitizer and disinfecting wipes, so we were lucky we didn't get sick. I did manage to come home with walking pneumonia, most likely from our trip to Xian where we saw the famous terracotta warriors. Our tour guide told us it is an arid place, and the dust in the air is laden with bacteria from the topsoil that blows around. We were cautioned to wear a surgical mask to avoid lung problems. After viewing the mind-boggling spectacle of the hundreds of unearthed, life-size terracotta figures, we were shuttled off to the food hall where lunch was being served. Naturally, we all wanted to use the facilities and then wash our hands after being in such a dusty climate, only to find no running water in the restrooms and only a pan of water and a dirty towel on a bench in the hallway.

One of the most memorable sights in China has to be the Great Wall. It is said that it's the only man-made structure that can be seen from outer space. Well, it certainly is impressive close up. We had an opportunity to walk on the wall and climb up to one of the many towers that connect each segment. As we walked back to our awaiting bus, we happened to walk past a bus that was filled with a group of Canadian high school students. One of them held out a small statue of a terracotta warrior, and mimicking a Chinese merchant shouted, "How much you pay?" The kids in the bus roared with laughter. I quickly responded, "I'll give you a Snickers for that!" His eyes lit up and he yelled, "You've got a deal!" After two weeks of eating Chinese food, this kid was drooling over the thought of getting a Snickers bar. As I was handing him the candy bar, his friend said to him, "You can't do that!" I quickly offered to sweeten the deal and throw in a Kit Kat, he nearly threw the statue at me. Later, on our bus, it was agreed that I made the best deal of the day.

We visited the Forbidden City, the Summer Palace, Tiananmen Square, Shanghai, the Ming tombs, and cruised on the Li River. It was always fun to travel with Mary because she looked at everything with childlike wonder. To Mary, life was a banquet and she never missed a morsel. You would think that a woman who flew around the world by herself could not possibly be impressed by new sights; not so with Mary. Even the most mundane aspect of life in China was fascinating to her. She played with the children in a Chinese commune one moment, and fed the chickens the next. Some of the young Chinese women would stand outside our tour bus and mimic applying lipstick. That was their way of asking for used tubes of lipstick, something not readily available to them. Mary gave away one or two to some very appreciative young girls.

I'll never forget the man who walked up to the bus as we were loading to leave the Great Wall. He had a piece of black construction paper in hand, and a pair of scissors. He would stand there and stare at you, then begin cutting the paper. His scissors worked their magic as bits of paper went flying, and within minutes he would hold up a perfect silhouette of you. It was uncanny!

The most Westernized city in China was Shanghai. It has wide boulevards lined with tall buildings, so England's colonial influence is quite obvious. There is a promenade along the river called the Strand, and it is a popular place for the local Chinese to stroll. Our group got off the bus and wandered along the Strand for a bit, then our tour guide challenged us. He wanted to see who could draw the biggest crowd of curious Chinese people. We already had a contingent of them following us, seemingly fascinated by our every movement. I said, "You're on," and promptly grabbed Mary and started doing the polka while singing, "Roll Out The Barrel." Suddenly, the crowd of ten Chinese turned into one hundred! They were laughing, clapping, and shouting, "Roll Out Barrel." I'm sure that our picture still graces the wall of some Chinese person's home in Shanghai to this day. We had great fun on the Strand.

In China in 1986, everyone made approximately $1 per day. It did not matter if you dug ditches for a living, or practiced brain surgery. It was a purely Communist system, so everyone shared in the misery. Today, government-condoned capitalism is the order of the day, and millionaires are springing up everywhere. When we visited Beijing, you could count the number of automobiles on one hand, and see a million bicycles. Today, automobiles are everywhere, and although bicycles are still prevalent, they are now competing with cars for the streets.

Mary, the travel agent, was in charge of optional excursions, and one she chose was a dinner cruise on the Li River. If you are familiar with those Chinese paintings that feature gumdrop-shaped mountains in the mist, surrounded by bamboo forests, that's the view along the Li River. It was absolutely spectacular.

We stood on the steps of our hotel waiting for our transfer to the pier, when Mary suddenly shrieked. I looked down to see what prompted her reaction and saw a large river rat, probably the size of a cat. It leisurely strolled across the step in front of us, then disappeared in the bushes adjacent to the staircase. Rodents were everywhere in China. As we later recounted our experience to our tour guide, he told us about a call from a hysterical member of his previous group. She was screaming into the phone about a mouse that was on her bureau nibbling on some crackers she brought along. He arrived at her room shortly thereafter, and found the door open, so he walked in and saw the woman on the bed, screaming that the mouse was on the bureau. But she didn't notice the large rat under her bed. He dispatched the mouse and then took her down for a drink to calm her down, never telling her about her rat problem!

Prior to our trip, a fellow travel agent advised us to take an old-fashioned, hard-sided Samsonite suitcase filled with peanut butter, crackers, tuna fish, candy bars, and other snacks. Puzzled by this, we asked her to explain. She remarked that aside from the government run food halls, there were no restaurants, so if you needed a snack between meals, there was literally no place to go. The hard sided luggage prevented the rats and mice from chewing through to get the food. The China of today is vastly different, with American fast-food restaurants, and finer dining available everywhere.

We leisurely cruised down the Li River in an oversized houseboat, stopping along the way for the chef to buy dinner...freshwater shrimp and some sort of fish. The fishermen who sold the chef his catch had a unique method of fishing. A man would be in a flimsy, wooden boat with two or more cormorants, a type of bird that dives for its dinner. The cormorants had a piece of rope tied around their throats, and a rope tied to one leg. The rope around the leg prevented them from escaping, and the rope around the throat prevented them from swallowing the fish they dove for. The fishermen would remove the fish when the bird surfaced, then sent him back for more. I'm sure it is a practice that goes back centuries.

We sat down for dinner and dined on the shrimp and other unrecognizable things, using our chopsticks that came in a paper wrapper marked, "Sanitized for your protection." Our mistake was taking a walk aft to see the kitchen facilities. There they were, two women washing the chopsticks in river water, then placing them in the wrappers. We bought our own chopsticks after that experience.

Other tours included a cloisonné factory, rug factory, jade factory, and a commune thrown in for good measure; the latter to impress the Westerners with the glory of Communism. It was all so very bleak in terms of working conditions, but the commune won the prize for the most bizarre.

With great pride, the guide showed us an acupuncture clinic and dentists office in the commune. Our eyes were wide as saucers as we witnessed an elderly woman with crippling rheumatoid arthritis being treated by a Chinese doctor. Into each swollen knuckle she had a rather large needle inserted, with a wad of smoldering cotton at the end. She smiled at us with rotten teeth, and did not seem to be in any pain.

Her horribly decayed teeth were understandable when we saw the dentist's office. It had an old white metal dentist chair with black cushions, not seen in the US since the fifties, and a Rube Goldberg array of pulleys and the horrific instruments to go with them. It looked like a medieval torture chamber. We both looked at each other and prayed we wouldn't get a toothache in China!

We were in Tiananmen Square one day, not knowing there would be a Democracy protest some years later, and that famous photo would appear with the brave Chinese man standing in front of a tank. The large portrait of Mao Tse Tung hovered over the square like Big Brother, and it gives one an eerie feeling of what life must be like under totalitarianism. Armed police were everywhere, and always keeping a keen eye on the Western tourists…as though we were going to spontaneously foment a revolution.

If anything, at that time, the culture needed a revolution in sanitation. The Chinese have a bad habit of spitting in public. Men, women, and children think nothing of hocking a loogie right on the sidewalk. And young parents allowed their toddlers to walk barefoot on the sidewalks, without diapers. The little ones wore pants that were split up the middle, so when the wee one got the urge to urinate or defecate, he or she simply lets it go. So, when walking down the street in Beijing, we had to sidestep sputum, urine, feces, and a host of other disgusting things. Now, I must remind you that this was in 1986, and after centuries of isolation from the West. An isolated society seems to take on certain habits that become commonplace and acceptable. I'm sure that some aboriginal societies in New Guinea practiced cannibalism until the missionaries showed up. I have to believe that some of things in China have changed for the good over the years since our honeymoon.

Needless to say, our honeymoon was an adventure, much like our life together.

12

Along Came a Spider

LIPSTICK RED

In August of 1986, we decided that it was time for Mary to get a new car. Her brown, 1974 Toyota Corolla was rather Spartan and had seen better days. Earlier that year, I had been in Milwaukee on a business trip and stayed downtown at the Adam's Mark Hotel. There happened to be a car on display in the lobby that caught my eye. It was an Alfa Romeo Spider Veloce, a cute little Italian roadster that looked like it was going ninety miles per hour just standing still. I told Mary about the car and suggested that perhaps it was time we upgraded her vehicle to one with carpeting and a little pizzazz. We drove over to the Alfa Romeo dealer in Maywood, Illinois, to take a look at the new models.

We walked into the showroom and there it was...a bright red Spider that Mary instantly fell in love with. Naturally, a rather arrogant salesman approached us as we looked at the sexy little sports car. It was the Spider model with the leather seats, canvas top, and other goodies that set it apart from the cheaper Graduate model (named after the little red Spider that Dustin Hoffman drove in the movie of the same name). The Spider Veloce stickered at a little more than $17,000 brand new. In today's market, a similar car would be twice as much. After driving one, we decided that we wanted the red one in the showroom. When it came down to playing the money game with the salesman, we were taken aback by his unwillingness to deal with us. His approach to it was simply this, "If you don't buy it, the next guy will." He would not budge off the sticker price. It was the affluent eighties and those cars were selling like hot cakes, plus, we may have let down our guard and were too effusive about how much we liked it. Being emotional about a vehicle is the worst possible thing to communicate to a car salesman. Lesson learned. Since then, I have never let a car salesman treat me that way; I am always ready to walk away from a vehicle if they won't meet my price. It's a winning formula that works every time. Bottom line: I wanted Mary to have that little car, so we drove it home that day.

It was probably the weekend after we bought the car that we decided to drive it out to Iowa to show Mary's folks. They must have wondered what their daughter had gotten herself into. She moved to Chicago, married this Italian boy, got a mink coat and a new Alfa Romeo, and now she's building a huge house. 1986 was one hell of a good year for us.

On occasion, Mary would drive the Alfa downtown to work. She'd pick up my brother-in-law's brother Tommy, and somehow managed to stuff the six-foot-tall man into that car, along with his cane and briefcase. Those two enjoyed riding together and became very close. Mary was very fond of Tommy, and admired him for his courage to overcome his handicap and go to work for the city every day, never complaining or feeling victimized. Somehow, I think Tommy inspired Mary and helped her deal with her lymphoma when she was diagnosed a few years later.

Sometimes Mary's wild streak overrode her sensible side. One day, I was outside on the driveway when Mary came home from work after dropping Tommy off at home a few blocks away. She had the top down and pulled up with a big smile on her face, and sucking the last few drops out of a longneck bottle of beer! I went ballistic and shouted, "What the hell is wrong with you? Where'd you get that beer? Are you crazy? Do you want a DUI and then lose your license? Oh, my God!" In her typical, nonplussed manner, she simply said, "Oh, piffle!" and shrugged it off. She went on to explain that she'd become friends with the young man who worked the pay station booth at the parking garage, and he offered her and Tommy a cold beer. Mary simply said, "It sounded so good!" as she sashayed into the yard after giving me a big kiss.

She was a rebel, whereas I always played by the book. If the sign said "Out," she went in. If it said "Up," she went down. It was as if rules were written for someone else, not her. When I'd try to correct her, she'd just dig her heels in deeper. Whenever she did that, I would picture her as a little girl, defiantly holding onto the arms of a chair as her dad tried to lift her out of it. By contrast, I was the goody two-shoes. I made left turns from the left turn lane, I used my turn signals religiously, and I never went in a door that said "Out." That makes my Virgo skin crawl. Mary teased me about my idiosyncrasies, but it was always in fun.

Mary loved that Alfa until the day she died, and I still drive it. I'll never be able to part with that car because it has such sentimental value to me. We did sell it once when we hit the road in our motor home. We sold it to friends of ours who lived near Des Moines because they always loved it and promised it a good home. Mary and I agreed to part with it, but with implicit instructions that if they ever wanted to sell it, we would have the first right to buy it back. Two years later, I received an email from Kim saying that she and Kevin were getting a divorce; did I want the car back? We bought it back and it has never left us since.

I used to tease Mary about driving the Alfa with the top down, while wearing a stylish scarf, big movie star sunglasses, and bright red nails and lipstick. I jokingly called it "whore red," and said she did that just so she could look like Katharine Hepburn and get whistled at. I now live in Palm Springs, California, and the joke is on me. Now I get whistled at!

And sorry, the Alfa is not for sale.

13

We Build Mary's Dream House

VILLA DIVIGGIANO AND OUR "LADY"

We were probably yuppies before they ever coined the phrase. We were both working in travel industry white-collar jobs, had no kids, lived in a building that I owned, and because it was the eighties, we were socking money away. We decided that living on busy Archer Avenue, with the city buses rumbling by and the airplanes flying overhead landing at Midway, was not our cup of tea. We began our hunt for a house. It began with Realtors showing us houses in the fashionable suburbs of LaGrange and Hinsdale. These are very affluent areas that are densely populated with professionals and office workers who commute daily by train to the Loop. Houses near the train station were at a premium price. Even in 1987 we were looking at "Handyman Specials" for over $200,000 because of the location. We decided that the western suburbs were out of our league and shifted our focus to the familiar southwest suburbs of Palos Hills, Palos Heights, and Palos Park (listed in ascending order of prestige). Palos Park was and is still one of the most prestigious south suburbs, so we never set our sights on houses there. We started in Palos Hills and looked at a number of what I call "sixties cookie-cutter houses". I think the crowning blow was the house with the doorbell that rang to the tune of "Zip-a-Dee-Doo-Dah," and the plastic runners on the carpets along with the plastic-covered furniture. We joked that the lady of the house probably cleaned the living room with a garden hose.

One summer day, as we were taking a leisurely Sunday drive through the Cook County Forest Preserves in our Alfa Romeo Spider, we happened upon a sign on an empty tract of land just beyond the southern edge of the forest. It read, "Coming Soon…Woodland Shores Custom Home Sites" and simply listed a phone number. Eureka! A place to build a new home and get what we want, plus, it has a Palos Park address! We called the number and made an appointment to speak to Dan at an address in nearby Evergreen Park. We drove up to the address and took a double take…it was a bowling alley. We thought he may have written down the wrong number, so we called him from our "bag phone" on the front seat (an early version of the cellphone). Dan answered and said that yes, he was in the bowling alley. We looked at each other and wondered what we were getting into.

We went inside to the bar and asked the bartender for Dan. He said, "I'm Dan, are you John and Mary?" There we stood, in a bowling alley, talking to a tall, thin, cigarette-smoking bartender about building a new house. It all turned out to be legitimate…Dan explained that his father-in-law, who owned the bowling alley, also owned this tract of land in unincorporated Palos Park, and asked his two sons-in-law to develop it. Dan pulled out the plat for the area and showed us the available lots. Builders had purchased a number of them, but there were still many available in the first phase of the project. We wanted a corner lot, and the only one left was a pie-shaped lot near the front of the development. It was slightly smaller and priced at $46,000. The one we really wanted was at the opposite end of that street. It was larger and a square corner, rather than a curve, and it was $48,000. Dan remarked that a builder of custom homes named Jim owned it. He was sure that Jim would be willing to build us a house on that lot. We put a deposit on the first one and got Jim's phone number.

Jim Marth was a thin, thirty-something building contractor who built about thirty homes a year. He was a pleasant fellow who had a very relaxed way of doing business. His office was in the basement of his home in nearby Lockport, Illinois, but our initial meeting with him took place in one of his model homes during a weekend open house. We walked into the home in the Oak Creek subdivision and there sat Jim behind a card table with two folding chairs. After exchanging pleasantries and taking a look at the model home, we agreed to sign a contract to build a house at 106 Whispering Lake Drive. As with most women, Mary loved the name of our street, but I never did. As a man, it sounded too prissy for my tastes. For God's sake, lakes don't whisper, they don't even talk! I wanted to adopt an address on the street our house paralleled...Lake Trail Drive, but the township prevailed and told us that we had to use the street on which the house fronted. I learned to accept the feminine nature of our street's name, and now I treasure the happy days we spent on Whispering Lake Drive.

Our first order of business was to choose a design for the house. Jim showed us some of the most popular elevations, and none of them appealed to us. We did not want to see our house style repeated on every block, so we stayed away from the ranch styles, the Georgians, and the split-levels. We took a ride one day and happened to turn down one of the streets about a mile from our home's site, and spotted a two-story, brick colonial home that made us both say, "Wow!"

The challenge was to find the architect's plan for this house and Jim's advice was to see the largest architect in the south suburbs. We drove down to their office and started looking through books that featured two-story homes. We opened the third book and there it was. The development's minimum square footage for a two story home was 2,800 square feet, and the style we were looking at was about 3,200. Cost was a factor for us, and 2,800 was our limit. Jim looked at the plan and showed us how he could pare down the house to 2,800 square feet and keep it within our budget. He knew that this was our first home and that we had to be careful with money, so he agreed to build our house with a $5,000 deposit. He never asked a nickel more from us until the closing, and for that we were always grateful.

We secured financing with Bell Federal Savings and locked in a 5.5 percent interest rate but we had to close by early November. That gave Jim less than two months to build our house, but he agreed to do it. Mind you, the neighborhood was nothing more than a dirt field with the streets marked by red flags, and the only sign of development was the fire hydrants and manhole covers. They dug out the basement and it proceeded to rain, and rain, and rain, quickly filling the hole with about three feet of water. Once the rain stopped and the hole was pumped out, the concrete contractor poured the footings and the foundation, and our home began to take shape. The framing began shortly thereafter and the first floor appeared in a day. From that point on, things happened quickly. We lived about thirty minutes from the site, so I drove out there every day to check on the progress.

At the time, we were trying to sell Mary's house in Iowa City, and we were not having much luck. The housing market in Iowa was depressed, and her house had some less than desirable features: a small backyard and small bedrooms. It was a pleasant little house but just a bit on the boring side. We eventually sold the home for slightly less than Mary paid for it, but it was done and we were relieved. We always joked because whenever we had a serious buyer, we'd add an upgrade to our new house, then, when that buyer fell through, we'd take something out. Our original budget of $180,000 wound up being $215,000 by the time we added landscaping and things like window treatments.

I always told Mary that she could have anything she wanted in that house as long as I could have a heated garage, with hot and cold running water, and a floor pitched to the center with a drain—the latter was against the building code, but Jim found a way to get it done without a problem. We spent hours looking at fixtures, lighting, brick, and ceramic tile. I always joked that any marriage that can survive building a house, can survive anything. We got into more arguments about tile than anything else. We had to choose tile for three bathrooms, the kitchen, and the foyer. I was pretty amenable to just about anything unless it was too gaudy. Mary and I had very similar tastes, but I quickly lost interest and when she'd ask me if I liked something, I'd respond, "Yes, it's okay." She'd snap back, "You don't like it, because if you did you'd say you really like it!" I couldn't win. We'd always wind up laughing about it afterward.

Jim finished the house on time and we moved in just before Thanksgiving 1987. We were the very first family to move into Woodland Shores, so the folks who followed called us the pioneers.

After living in the city all my life, you can imagine my delight when I looked out the family room bay window on a frosty December morning, just before Christmas, and saw a solitary rider on his horse, coming down the unpaved street. I knew my life was going to be different now. There I was, standing in my magnificent new suburban home, seeing a sight I'd never seen before. I called Mary over to witness the scene, and there we stood in the window, embracing each other and reveling in the moment. I can vividly remember the crackle of the fire in the fireplace and thinking about what we had accomplished together.

Mary was in "hog heaven" in her new home. It was a great source of pride for both of us, in that two thirty-somethings from humble backgrounds, could live in a brand-new custom home in prestigious Palos Park. Being the talented seamstress she was, Mary proceeded to make all of the window coverings...swags, Roman shades, and sheers. They turned out great and saved us thousands of dollars. Her tastes in wallpaper and her willingness to use color made the house elegant and appealing. We bought furniture for the living room by finding pieces in the "scratch and dent" sections, but no one was ever the wiser. We furnished our family room with mission style leather furniture reminiscent of Frank Lloyd Wright, and used a similar style in our kitchen. It was a wonderful home that suited us well and turned out to be a terrific investment.

We planned various projects for the home, many of which were focused on the inside and accomplished that winter, but when spring arrived, I told Mary that we couldn't spend another nickel on the inside, until the outside was finished. I said, "We need to make it look like we can afford to live here...so we can't do another thing indoors until the landscaping is completed!" Little did I know that as far as Mary was concerned, landscaping is an ongoing project, one that is *never* finished! That's what I get for marrying the farmer's daughter, one who loves to have her hands in the dirt.

Mary poured over magazines and planned the look of the yard, then changed it, and changed it again and again. I must say that our backyard resembled an English garden, with flowers that bloomed every spring, summer, and fall. We planted trees, a hedge of arbor vitae instead of a fence, a Washington hawthorne ornamental tree outside our family room window, a flagstone patio in one corner of the yard, and a paving brick patio adjacent to the house. Naturally, I had to add my touches to the yard to make it special, including a purple martin birdhouse and a large flagpole. The purple martin house was my first line of defense against the mosquitoes that plagued us in the summer. Purple martins are the largest of the swallow family, and each bird consumes approximately two thousand mosquitoes per day! I had a permanent nesting colony that returned every year from their winter home in Brazil. Mary and I would spend hours on our patio, lying in the hammock, watching the purple martins swoop and dive, eating all those pesky mosquitoes! Their song would greet us every morning, and every year I would replace a nestling or two that had fallen out of the house. I truly became the birdman of Whispering Lake Drive.

What I didn't realize is that most of the mosquitoes come out after the purple martins go to sleep, so I was on a quest to find the missing link. It did not take long…bats! I did my research and found that our area was the summer home of the little brown bat, aka *Myotis lucifugus*. These remarkable creatures eat several times their weight each night in harmful insects. They would come out at dusk, swooping and flying around, gorging themselves on mosquitoes, moths, mayflies, and all sorts of pesky insects. I was so enamored with bats; I purchased a bat house and mounted it on the side of our home. At first, Mary thought I'd lost my mind because she bought into all those old wives tales about bats being blind and getting tangled in your hair. I assured her that none of that was true, and that bats have no higher rates of rabies than do raccoons or skunks, both of which populated the area. Bats suffer from a terrible reputation, so I became their self-appointed spokesperson and remain that today!

With our purple martin house, bat house, flagpole, and our English gardens, we rather stood out in the crowd as having one of the more interesting houses in Woodland Shores. We would never have won the "most-tacky" award, however. That title was reserved for our neighbors across the street, with Venus De Milo amid pier pilings and rope.

I always considered our home to be a work in progress, because just when I thought we were done, Mary would come up with a new project. If I could not do something myself, Mary was always ready to hire a contractor…and Mary had a knack for making men do her bidding. Whenever we were talking to a contractor about one of her projects, and he would say, "I can't do that, lady," Mary would respond with, "Sure you can; I have every faith in you,", or something to that effect. Just like the contractors in Iowa, somehow, with her charm and powers of persuasion, she could get anyone to do what she wanted. She was fun to watch when she was in rare form. She had a way about her that just made a man want to do things for her. She certainly had that effect on me.

On one of our many trips to Iowa to visit Mary's parents, her sister Jane knew that I loved dogs and mentioned that the local feed store had some cocker spaniel puppies for sale. I asked Mary if we could go there and look, to which she replied, "Yes, but we're just looking!" Having grown up on a farm, Mary considered dogs to be livestock, which belonged outside and not living in your house. I grew up in the city of Chicago and we always had dogs indoors. We went over to the feed store and they had two adorable, parti-colored cockers, a brother and sister. I picked up the female and I immediately fell in love. I said, "I want this one!" Mary replied, "Now, John, I said we were just going to look." I shot back, "I'm tired of just looking! I'm almost forty and if I want a puppy, I'm going to get one!" Mary looked at me wide-eyed and said, "Okay, honey, okay." Once we separated the two pups, they both started to cry, which tore my heart out. But I wasn't about to push my luck and say I wanted both of them. To this day, I regret not buying her brother—they would have been a cute pair. We drove home with Mary holding the pup, which promptly peed on her. I named her Lady, after *Lady and The Tramp*, a childhood favorite movie of mine. Her official AKC name was Lady Amelia Whitaker, after Mary's mom and Aunt Helen Whitaker (whose antique Eastlake style bedroom set graced one of our guest rooms).

We decided to kennel train Lady, so she was tucked into her kennel downstairs in the kitchen the first night, along with a hot water bottle and a ticking clock to comfort her. Well, I awoke in the middle of the night and there was no Mary in bed beside me. I went downstairs to the kitchen, and found Mary curled up on a makeshift bed on the floor next to Lady's kennel.

"She was crying," Mary stated, half asleep. From that point on, Mary was crazy about that little dog. Lady was a wonderful companion and returned the favor to Mary many times over, comforting her for the next twelve and a half years, through some of the worst periods of illness you can imagine.

It broke our hearts when we had to put lady down in 2002, but we showed her one last act of kindness, by ending her suffering. It was the very least we could do for our faithful companion, but it wasn't without shedding torrents of tears. Our veterinarian gave Lady the lethal injection that stopped her little heart outdoors, on a grassy knoll, under a swaying palm tree as she lay comfortably cradled in my arms.

14

Supersonic wife of John

FLYING THE CONCORDE

Mary accepted a position with Thomas Cook Travel in Chicago and began working for them immediately after relocating from Iowa City. She was manager of their huge business travel center in the Equitable Building at Michigan Avenue and the Chicago River, directly across the street from the famous Wrigley Building. After coming from a small town AAA Travel office, she thrived in the bustling atmosphere of that busy urban travel center. In the 1980s, prior to computer conferencing, heightened airline security, and all other factors that affect travel today, major corporations bought airline tickets frequently for business travel. Consequently, Thomas Cook's volume of airline ticket sales was huge with the transatlantic carriers like British Airways, Air France, and others. The airline reps would come into her office and beg Mary to accept free, first or business class tickets to Europe. She couldn't possibly use them all so Mary used them as an incentive to motivate her employees. We still managed to fly frequently to Paris and London for the weekend to shop or just go to the theater. Air France invited Mary twice to join a select group of top-producing travel agency managers on a five-day trip to Paris via the Concorde. She turned them down each time because I could not go along. The third time they asked I told her that she *had* to accept the invitation so I could live vicariously through her. Mary promised me that she would accept the invitation if it were offered to her again. It was, and on February 16, 1988, Mary boarded a flight to New York City where she connected to AF Flight 02, non-stop service to Paris on the Concorde.

The flight took three hours and twenty minutes to cross the Atlantic at speeds that reached Mach 1, over 1,300 miles per hour, which is literally faster than a bullet out of the barrel of a gun. The now-retired aircraft was an engineering marvel. It was capable of cruising at supersonic speeds at an altitude of 60,000 feet, nearly twice as high as conventional subsonic commercial aircraft. At that altitude, it's possible to see the curvature of the Earth and stars up above. The tremendous friction caused by the air rushing past the fuselage causes the exterior skin of the aircraft to heat up. Mary reported that the tiny windows were actually warm to the touch despite the -60F temperature of the outside air. The delta shaped wings that make supersonic flight possible required an odd take-off and landing posture for the aircraft. It ascended and descended at a rather acute angle (much like the space shuttle), requiring a drop-down nose so the pilot had a clear view of the runway on final approach. Aside from that aspect, and the narrow interior, it felt like any other commercial aircraft, except when it broke the sound barrier. Mary told me that as the plane approached the sound barrier, it began to shudder ever so slightly. It did so for a few seconds, then, as if going from a cobblestone road to a paved surface, it became as smooth as glass. The only sensation of movement was the sound of the air rushing past the fuselage.

After the food service, which was French gourmet, Mary, in her own inimitable way, talked her way into the cockpit during supersonic flight. I have photos of Mary standing in the cockpit and smiling with the pilot and copilot while the aircraft was cruising at twice the speed of sound. They gave her a certificate stating that Mary, "Supersonic wife of John", broke the sound barrier on the Concorde on the 16th of February 1988. She was a supersonic wife, in more ways than one.

Upon arrival in Paris, Mary and her small group of prominent Chicago travel agents were met at De Gaulle Airport and driven to their hotel in a stretch Mercedes limousine. Air France spared no expense and arranged accommodations at the famous Hotel de Crillon at the Place de la Concorde. This famous French luxury hotel is adjacent to the American Embassy and overlooks the famous Egyptian obelisk from Luxor, Egypt, that stands in the epicenter of the Place de la Concorde. Even in 1988, the hotel rooms were more than $500 per night at this luxurious property, and each travel agent had his or her own private room, complimentary, of course. The next few days were filled with private-car sightseeing, lavish dinners, and plenty of French champagne. The Air France folks weren't going to let this trip become anti-climactic, so the flight home was in the First Class cabin on a 747.

While Mary was in Paris, I decided that I wanted to do something fun for her upcoming fortieth birthday on the fifth of May. Her trip to Paris gave me the opportunity to do something exciting and spontaneous. Mary played the piano beautifully, but we did not have one at that time. We had just moved into our new home a little over a year prior, and we still did not have all our furniture, so I decided to buy her a baby grand piano for her birthday. I went out to a large piano retailer in Chicago, admittedly knowing nothing about them and bought a beautiful, high gloss ebony Korean brand. I would normally have done some research, but I had to have it in the house when she arrived home from her trip. The piano I bought was probably not the best to a piano aficionado, but it had many of the features of the expensive Yamahas and Baldwins, at one-third the price, plus, it could be delivered in time for her return home.

I picked her up at O'Hare Airport and heard all about the Concorde and Paris on the ride home. When we got there, Mary was so happy to be back in her new house, she wandered through it just looking at each room thinking about furniture and window treatments. As she moved into the living room with me right behind, she turned the corner from the dining room and stopped cold in her tracks. She didn't say a word, she just put her hands on her cheeks and turned to me with her mouth wide open, speechless. I simply said, "Happy fortieth birthday, sweetheart, and welcome home." She wrapped her arms around my neck, gave me a big kiss, and said, "John, you shouldn't have done this," then sat down and began to play. She looked like an angel sitting there playing that piano with the vase of long-stemmed red roses sitting on top. She stopped a few times and asked about how much it cost, but each time I encouraged her to play, telling her that I'd fill her in later.

Little did we know that a malignant disease was growing inside her as she sat there playing Chopin's Polonaise, Opus 53 in A flat major.

15

Diagnosis: Cancer

TICKLES, COUGHS, AND CURLING IRONS

This chapter contains the most poignant and challenging aspect of our life together: Mary's diagnosis with non-Hodgkin's lymphoma in early 1989.

After Mary returned from Paris she began to notice an annoying tickle in her throat and a nagging cough that just would not go away. It was particularly noticeable when she would bend forward or raise her hands to put on a blouse—a vague presence in her throat. We decided to have an ear, nose, and throat physician take a look at her. My ENT physician, Dr. Gavron was on vacation and had a female doctor covering for him. She looked in Mary's throat and palpated her neck and upper chest. She asked Mary if she used a curling iron, to which Mary replied, "Yes." "You have some enlarged lymph nodes in your neck, probably due to the use of the curling iron," she said. Our response was, "Please explain." She went on to say that using a curling iron could cause a low-grade infection that can enlarge the lymph glands…nothing to worry about. She sent us home with a prescription for an antibiotic and discouraged the use of the curling iron.

Mary stayed busy working downtown and by making the window treatments that adorned every room in our house. She still had the tickle in her throat and the cough that accompanied it. I have suffered from allergies most of my adult life, so I attributed her problem to living in the suburbs near the Cook County Forest Preserves. The problem was, the symptoms continued into the winter, and just after the first of the year, Mary was putting on makeup in the morning and noticed a lump in front of her left earlobe. She pointed it out to me and I told her that we needed to go back and see Dr. Gavron. We made an appointment and saw him within the week. He examined her and told us that the enlarged parotid (salivary) gland was due most likely to a benign condition called sarcoidosis, a common ailment in women that causes glands in the body to enlarge. To be certain, he arranged for surgery to have it removed. He would do the surgery because of the delicate nature of its location near the facial nerve.

The surgery was scheduled for February 20, 1989, her parents' wedding anniversary. It was to be done at our local hospital, Palos Community Hospital in Palos Heights, just ten minutes from our house. An old friend of mine, Carol, was the head of the surgical nursing staff at the time, and her friend Dana was a surgical nurse at Palos Community. The girls made Mary feel very comfortable, since they would be assisting Dr. Gavron through the surgery. They were with us during the pre-surgical prep period and Dana assisted during the procedure. I stayed in pre-op and held Mary's hand until they administered the first of the anesthesia. Little did I know that this was the first of many surgeries I would see her through. She had been my wife for less than two years. When I left to go back to the waiting room, Dana and Carol sat with her until she went under. A pre-op chest X-ray was done and Mary told me later that while she was in twilight, she overhead the doctors who were reviewing the X-ray say "lymphoma," then she fell asleep. The pre-op X-ray showed a large mass in the mediastinum area, surrounding the thyroid gland. This mass accounted for the discomfort and the cough that Mary had been suffering for nearly a year. When she bent forward or raised her arms the tumor would exert pressure on her trachea and trigger the cough.

The surgery went well, despite the fact that the tumor was intertwined around the facial nerve, requiring some very delicate surgical skill. After the surgery, Dr. Gavron met with us in a small consultation room. Mary's mom, dad, Carol, Dana, Phyllis, and I were all gathered there, knowing by the look on the faces of the doctor and our friends that the news was not good. He proceeded to tell us that the surgery went well, that Mary was doing fine, but that the frozen section biopsy done immediately indicated that Mary had non-Hodgkin's lymphoma, a cancer of the lymphatic system. Further pathology would be needed to stage the disease, and other tests, such as CAT scans, and MRIs were necessary to find other tumors. The mass in her chest seemed to be the biggest concentration of the cancer, but it could be elsewhere. We decided that we would not tell Mary right away so that she could get a good night's rest. We asked a few questions about any damage to the facial nerve and he assured us that it was intact and not to worry. He left the room and left us numb. We all looked at each other and the tears started to flow. I was devastated. It took me nearly thirty years to find my true love, and now a doctor had just told me that she had a life-threatening illness. I shed the first of many tears over the woman I loved.

I kissed her goodnight early in the evening because she was still groggy from the anesthesia and fighting to stay awake. I promised her that I would come back with the family in the morning. The phone rang about 8:00 a.m. the following morning and Mary's cheery voice was on the other end. She said, "Good morning, sweetheart. Why don't you come down here right now, Dr. Gavron is here. He told me, and I'm okay, but I want you here now." I could sense the fear in her voice. I said, "I'm on my way," and slammed the phone down. I jumped out of bed and yelled, "Shit! Why did he have to tell her before I got there! Dammit!" I was furious that he delivered the bad news without me being there, when I specifically told him not to.

I raced down to the hospital leaving the in-laws to fend for themselves. I ran up to Mary's room to find that Dr. Gavron was still there, sitting on the edge of her bed holding her hand. He was softly reassuring her that she was going to be okay and she was just beaming at him. I called out to her and she turned her head toward me. She said, "Hi, honey. It's okay. I'm okay. Dr. Gavron told me everything." I shot him a dirty look but said nothing to him. I turned to Mary and said, "He was supposed to wait until I got here." She replied, "It's okay, honey, I made him tell me because I heard the word *lymphoma* just before I fell asleep in pre-op." It became clear to me that Mary was a woman who didn't want anything sugarcoated…she needed the facts. The doctor said he was waiting for the pathology report, asked if we had an oncologist, apologized for betraying our pact, and left us to make his rounds. Mary just lay there beaming her beautiful smile at me, and simply said, "I love you." I grasped her hand in mine and responded, "I love you too, honey, but with that gauze wrapped around your head, it looks like you're ready to raise your fist and yell, 'Death to America!' We both just burst into laughter. There we were, facing the fight of our lives, and laughing like little kids. Humor served us well during the nearly eighteen years we fought that insidious disease.

Dr. Gavron referred us to a staff oncologist, whose name I have blocked from my memory because of his cold, detached manner. A few days later we were to meet with him in his hospital office to find out what we were dealing with. They sent an orderly with a wheelchair to take Mary down to the office at the appointed time. We sat there and waited patiently for the doctor who arrived shortly thereafter with a file folder in his hands. He introduced himself and sat down opening the folder. In a very cold and clinical fashion, he began. I sat there with a pen and legal pad while Mary sat there blankly staring at him. My hand was shaking so badly I could hardly write.

"You have low-grade, small-cell, indolent non-Hodgkin's lymphoma. The primary mass is centered in the mediastinum and various lymph nodes in the neck and facial areas." I was trying to take everything down in a chicken scratch manner of handwriting. The Dominican nun's efforts to make the Palmer Method of handwriting stick were a dismal failure at that moment. I wrote much like a doctor that day. He continued telling us about the old and new methods of typing the disease, and started to explain treatment options, one of which is "wait and see." Mary continued to stare blankly and then uttered, "How long do I have?" His response, which felt like a knife to the heart, was so flippant and insensitive that I've tried to block it from my mind ever since. He leaned back in his chair, put his hands behind his head and said, "You have seven to ten years…go home and have a beer." I dropped my pen and looked over at Mary, she was boring a hole in him with her eyes and simply said, "All right…let's get started."

They kept her in the hospital overnight so I drove home alone, sobbing uncontrollably. There I was, married less than two years to the love of my life, had just built her a brand new home, and now I was practically picking out caskets.

I brought Mary home the next day with a prescription for chlorambucil, a chemotherapy drug in pill form. It was one of the oldest and most effective treatments for low-grade lymphomas at that time. It is an alkalizing agent that destroys white blood cells, and it was discovered quite by accident. The key ingredient is the substance used in mustard gas, the deadly gas used against the allies in WWI. Doctors discovered low white cell counts in dough boys exposed to the gas in the trenches. It was later found to be effective in fighting lymphomas.

I will never forget the day Mary took that very first pill. She was seated on our family room sofa, Phyllis and Jane on either side of her. I handed her the pill and a glass of water, and she held that pill up as if it were the sacred Host at a Catholic mass. The tears were flowing as she swallowed that pill and vowed that it was going to work. It may have been at that point when she uttered her famous phrase, "I can't die…I don't want some slut sleeping on my side of the bed!" The tears quickly turned to laughter.

The pill did work. Her tumor shrank and proved that low-grade lymphoma tends to respond to everything, it just doesn't stay away. Indolent lymphomas are notorious for relapsing. If memory serves, Mary took the chlorambucil but never again saw that oncologist who instructed her to "have a beer." Unbeknownst to us, our friends Carol and Dana were canvassing the medical staff at Palos Community to find us another oncologist. The name that surfaced most often amongst med students and doctors alike was Dr. Margaret Telfer of the University of Illinois and Michael Reese Hospitals. She was a professor of hematology-oncology at the University of Illinois, and considered a foremost authority on lymphomas. That was enough for us.

We made an appointment to see Dr. Telfer and liked her immediately. Dr. Peggy, as Mary came to call her, is a single woman from a large Catholic family. She was a walking, talking textbook on the subject of lymphoma and sickle cell anemia. She lived in Hyde Park, a fashionable neighborhood near the University of Chicago. In her calm, retiring, soft-spoken manner, Dr. Peggy told us immediately to forget the statistics we've heard regarding life expectancies. She said, "Those statistics are seven to ten years old… people live with lymphomas for decades, and new treatments are coming out practically every day." Those words alone lifted the weight of the world off our shoulders. Her sweet, sensitive, and caring manner made us feel like everything was going to be okay.

She was of the opinion that we needed to gain some ground and use a more aggressive treatment in the hopes we can attain remission. It was agreed that we would begin CHOP therapy, a chemo cocktail of Cytoxan, Adriamycin, vincristine, and prednisone.

Dr. Telfer's chemotherapy nurse specialist was Anita Bontuyan, a charming lady originally from the Philippines. She, too, was single and lived right across the street from Michael Reese Hospital. Like most of the people associated with Mary's treatment at Michael Reese, we came to love Anita. Her kindness and caring manner, her deep faith in God, and her knowledge of the various treatments always put us at ease when Mary would come in for a treatment. I made it a point to be with Mary whenever I could, but when I could not, I was comforted to know that she was under the care of Dr. Telfer and Anita at the Michael Reese hematology-oncology clinic.

Whenever we had an appointment to see Dr. Telfer or for a treatment, we never sat in the waiting room. Anita would immediately usher us into a treatment room, make Mary comfortable, and wait on me like I was the King of England. Anita loved my sense of humor, and it wasn't difficult to make her laugh. Her giggle was infectious, and her love for Mary was obvious. Everyone at the clinic was fond of Mary and enjoyed having her there. It was unfortunate that she had to be there for cancer treatment, but better there than somewhere else. In a way, we became spoiled by the preferential treatment we received at the clinic, and were taken aback when we had to go elsewhere once we moved away from Chicago. They made us wait...they didn't have Cokes, or candy, or popcorn, or crackers for us to munch on... and they didn't laugh at my jokes! It was awful not going to the Michael Reese clinic anymore!

We were warned that CHOP therapy, although effective, was fraught with unpleasant side effects. The hair loss, nausea, vomiting, metallic taste in the mouth, mouth sores, and diarrhea were all too real. Mary was traumatized when she lost her strawberry blonde hair for the first time; it came out in large clumps and filled the sink. After brushing out all the loose hair, we stood in front of the large bathroom mirror. I remarked, "This makes you look like you're sick, why don't we just shave it all off?" Mary agreed so I did just that. She didn't look sick afterward, she looked cute. She wasn't crazy about going without hair in public, so I bought her an expensive, human-hair wig to wear to work. She did so and looked great. I offered to shave my head so she wouldn't feel as bad about losing hers, but she would not hear of it. As she ran her fingers through my hair she said, "I'm not going to let you shave off this gorgeous, wavy Italian hair!" I responded, "I suppose you're right, I'd look like Dumbo!" We always found a way to make light of a serious situation. In a way, it preserved our sanity.

The nausea was another matter. My cheerful, upbeat, wonderful girl suffered so. I would kneel next to her and hold her head as she vomited from the chemotherapy. Most of the time she didn't have anything in her stomach to regurgitate, so it was what we'd call the dry heaves. It was painful to watch, and downright unpleasant, but I never got sick to my stomach. I cleaned up after her, and made her comfortable when she finished, then I'd say something like, "I think I'll review my marriage vows and see where this fits in." She'd always smile and thank me for taking such good care of her. I always did, and it was always out of love. I couldn't stand to see my girl suffer so, and it made me so damn mad that she had to endure it.

I've heard stories of spouses who simply leave because of illness or suffering because *they* couldn't handle it. Well, I can't imagine anyone having to go through what Mary did, alone. When you truly love someone, you don't care what you have to do to spare your beloved one moment of suffering or pain. How a person can walk away in a situation like that is beyond my comprehension. If I could have traded places with her, I would have. That's how much I loved her.

Her first course of CHOP was effective and put her lymphoma into remission, for a time. Mary took a position with another business travel company, an agency with its home office in Omaha, Nebraska. She managed their large business travel center in the Prudential Building, in downtown Chicago. She was office manager and an interim City Manager, a position she was eminently qualified for, and one for which she had applied.

Much to her surprise, they chose a twenty-nine-year old man from the home office because he was raised in the "culture," whereas Mary gained her knowledge and expertise from working at a number of distinguished travel companies. The new "kid" was just that, and Mary had a habit of making him look bad at staff meetings. Not because she consciously tried to, she simply could run rings around him because he was so wet behind the ears.

16

You're Fired

THE MAIDS OF OAK LAWN

Her new boss had a habit of showing up at the office when he felt like it, so he had no clue what was going on. He was too busy handing in large expense account items like limousines and champagne. During a staff meeting something was brought up about a major account. His answer was so out of touch and ridiculous, Mary could not contain her laughter. That was the nail in her coffin when it came to that job.

Not surprisingly, he fired her the next day; something about insubordination. In hindsight, a middle-aged female cancer patient, dismissed without documented incidents could probably have mounted a legal challenge and won. We thought about it, but after enduring chemotherapy, it wasn't worth the aggravation. That, effectively, was the end of Mary's distinguished travel career.

The corporate travel industry was beginning to feel the pinch from lower airline commissions and a decrease in business travel. It was the early nineties and computer technology, the Internet, and higher fuel prices were all factors in this decline. Mary could see the handwriting on the wall, so she decided that she did not want to go back into corporate travel.

We knew that Mary wasn't the type to sit home all day with nothing to do, so we brainstormed about what new career she could pursue, knowing full well that her health was a factor. Our accountant, Leon, who worked magic with a tax form, advised us that we should consider buying a business for the tax benefits. A business, eh? We decided that that wasn't a bad idea so we contacted a business broker to test the waters. We registered with one in the southwest suburbs who was familiar with the area. His first question to us was, "Do you care what others think about how you earn a living?" My answer was that we'd buy a porno bookstore if it made us money, but Mary was less eager to do that. Naturally, I was half-joking when I said it, but I could understand his reason for asking. It turned out that there were so many businesses for sale, he was trying to weed out the ones that he knew we'd find undesirable. One of the businesses that caught my eye was a quick oil change shop, partly due to my interest in cars, and also because of their rise in popularity. Unfortunately, a start-up franchise was far too costly, and way too risky. Our pockets simply were not deep enough to open and support a new business until it was in the black. We needed to look at an affordable existing business, one that was either currently making money or had the potential to with our expertise. It also had to be a business that Mary could run, since I planned to keep my job with Pleasant Hawaiian Holidays and the benefits that came with it, especially given Mary's medical history.

After looking at several businesses, we found one that appealed to both of us…it was The Maids of Oak Lawn, a residential cleaning franchise, also based in Omaha, Nebraska. A middle-aged woman, who was struggling and wanted out, owned the business. After doing our due diligence, we made an offer and negotiated a price that we could all live with. For about $50,000 we had a business complete with all the equipment necessary to do the job. The work force was in place and the business had just been relocated to Oak Lawn, Illinois. We made arrangements for financing through my neighborhood credit union and set a closing date. It happened to fall on a date that had me in Hawaii on business, so we set up the necessary powers of attorney to allow Mary to close without me being present. We spoke via telephone the night before closing, and Mary expressed her trepidation about the decision and her wish that I were there to sign with her. I eased

her fears by saying, "Mary, if we don't do this now, we'll never do it." She never forgot those words and thanked me frequently over the years. She always admired my "no fear" attitude, so when I said everything was going to be okay, that was enough for her. She signed the papers the next day, and when I arrived back in Chicago, we were small business owners.

Despite the records the former owner made available to us, the picture was not as rosy as she made it out to be. We knew that the equipment was in a sorry state, broken vacuums, dirty cleaning rags, company cars filled with dents and needing paint, but we didn't realize that she was so desperate to stay afloat she woefully underpriced her cleaning services. Mary immediately worked on raising the quality of our work, and then the prices. We lost some accounts, but in many cases we could have paid the customer instead of cleaning her house and saved a lot of money.

Our franchise had a scientific method of cleaning that was based on efficiency and time management. A team of four uniformed, insured, bonded cleaning ladies were able to do a maintenance clean of a four bedroom house in about one hour. When we bought the business, our average cleaning price was probably about $70, so Mary worked hard to raise that average in the years that followed. In a short period of time, Mary raised the quality of the work, upgraded the equipment, and concentrated on replacing the employees who were unreliable or simply could not clean to The Maids' standards. When we sold the business six years later, the average clean had doubled, and the employees grew to love their boss.

We had one star employee from the day we bought the business; her name was Stephanie, a sweet woman in her mid-thirties who had a hard life but knew her job inside and out. She and Mary instantly bonded, and Stephanie worked for Mary until the day we sold the business. Stephanie made a series of bad choices in her life, but I think she blessed the day she decided to work for Mary DiViggiano. Her husband was in jail and her son was constantly in trouble with the police. At the time we met her, she was living with an abusive man who drank heavily and beat her mercilessly. There were many times she'd arrive at work with bruises or a black eye, or just didn't show up. It came to a point where the beatings were so frequent, and so severe, that Mary had to do something before he killed Stephanie. One day Mary answered a call in the morning and it was Stephanie whispering in the phone that she could not come into work because her boyfriend came home drunk and beat her badly. Mary was beside herself with

worry, so she told some of our employees what happened. Several of them piled into our company car, metal vacuum wand extensions in hand, and drove to Stephanie's place to pick her up and get her away from him. In the meantime, Mary was on the phone to a shelter for abused and battered women. She personally drove Stephanie and registered her at the shelter, ending her suffering at the hand of her sadistic boyfriend.

Mary threw herself headlong into the business and quickly turned a profit. She eventually turned the staff into a formidable cleaning machine, and I brought the cars and equipment up to standards while still working in the Hawaii travel business. I wore a Hawaiian shirt by day and wielded a screwdriver in the evening. We were busy, but our success came at a price.

THE MAD HATTER - 124½ E. WASHINGTON ST. - IOWA CITY, IOWA

The Mad Hatter Tea Room circa 1950's

Paris, France circa 1980

On our honeymoon in China, June 1986

Our Palos Park, IL home & "Lady" circa 1990

The Author and his "Mistress" circa 1995

Mary, "Lady", and me with the Rolls circa 1995

Mary and me with our Motorhome circa 2003

The Author and Mary at Outdoor Resort circa 2006

President Bush signing The Medicare Modernization
Bill as Mary looks on (upper right)

Renewing our Wedding Vows Feb. 14, 2003

17

La Vie En Rose

PLACES IN THE HEART

Less than a year after we bought the business and relocated it to a larger office, the lymphoma returned with a vengeance. Dr. Telfer asked us to meet with her and discuss treatment options. Mary's disease had relapsed a number of times, and with greater frequency, a sign that the histology of the lymphoma had changed, making it more aggressive. We sat there holding hands and listened intently as Dr. Telfer explained the available treatment options and suggested we see her associate, Dr. Rosalind Catchatourian, head of the bone marrow transplantation program at Michael Reese Hospital. She made it clear that a bone marrow transplant was our best chance for a cure, and went on to explain the risks involved, citing morbidity studies and statistics regarding survival rates. It was the classic risk/rewards approach that helps a patient make an informed decision.

As I think back, I can see that there sat a distinguished professor-physician delivering very sobering news to two informed adults who were acutely aware of the ramifications. I wondered how many people listened to her in the past and had absolutely no idea what she was talking about. It must be like having a diagnosis delivered to you in a foreign language. From the moment we learned Mary had lymphoma, we did the research necessary to learn all we could about this new adversary. The old adage is true…knowledge is power. Unfortunately, far too many people subscribe to the other adage…ignorance is bliss. It always amazed us when we'd speak to patients in a waiting room who did not know what type of cancer he or she had, or the type of treatment protocol they were about to be hooked up to for several hours. I firmly believe people like that do not fare as well against their disease. We learned early on that you cannot place your blind faith in doctors. That's not to say that we didn't have some amazing doctors, but you, the patient, must be in charge of your health care to the largest extent possible. By that, I mean you must question everything and not accept less than the best in medical care and treatment. It's your life.

We sat there for a few moments trying to process all the information we were just given, then looked at each other and smiled. Without saying a word, we knew what our answer would be. As memory serves, I believe Mary spoke first saying, "Dr. Telfer, I love my Johnny so much I can't stand the thought of leaving him alone. I want to do whatever it takes to live and if that means a bone marrow transplant, so be it." I could see the tears welling up in Dr. Telfer's eyes as I added, "Dr. Telfer, it took me nearly thirty years to find Mary, and I'm not willing to let her go…I think we decided a long time ago that we would do whatever it takes to beat this thing, as long as we can do it together." Dr. Telfer dabbed at her tears and gave each of us a hug, assuring us that Dr. Catchatourian was highly regarded in her field.

Dr. Rose, as Mary addressed her, was a cheerful, unassuming, delightful woman of Armenian descent who we instantly bonded with and grew to love. To this day, she remains a dear friend of mine. Rose loved Mary and the feeling was mutual. This woman of small stature, was less than five feet tall, but was a giant in her field. She is an accomplished hematology-oncology specialist who trained at the Hutchinson Cancer Center in Seattle and performed the first bone marrow transplant in Chicago back in the early eighties. She was born in India of Armenian parents, and worked with Mother Teresa for a time in Calcutta. She attended medical school in Taiwan. We instantly responded to her smiling face and charming demeanor; she had a way of instilling confidence with her smile and reassuring manner.

We talked about the two types of transplants available, an analogous transplant using donor marrow, and an autologous peripheral stem cell rescue using the patient's own stem cells harvested through a process called apheresis. Stem cells are immature cells that can develop into red, white, or platelet cells as needed by the body. Peripheral stem cells float freely in the blood and are easily harvested. Stem cells have been in the news lately, associated with research aimed at curing many dreaded diseases and conditions. Research is promising, though far from convincing, but their role in transplantation is proven and widely used. Each type of transplant involves risks, one of them being death. Back then, about one-third of transplant patients did not survive the treatment, most of them succumbing to infection.

Once again, we had to process an enormous amount of medical information but it was an easy decision to make. Mary wanted to live, and live she did. We immediately had all of her sisters tested for a match, but unfortunately, none did. I too was tested but the chance of a match was next to impossible. It was decided that we'd do a stem cell transplant and moved forward.

The transplant would follow weeks of apheresis and chemotherapy to clean up any active lymphoma. Mary made regular monthly trips to Michael Reese for the two-hour sessions to harvest her stem cells. The nurse/apheresis technician was Eileen, a cheerful single woman who loved her Old English sheepdog. Her charming personality and sense of humor made the sessions very pleasant, and she had quite a library of videotapes. I always looked forward to donating platelets because it was my opportunity to help other patients as well as Mary, and to watch the adventure films that Mary hated. On a number of occasions, Mary's dad would drive in from Iowa and accompany Mary to her sessions when I was in Hawaii or on a sales trip. Mel and Joe probably felt as helpless as I did at times, and the only way they could help was to be there for Mary when she needed them. Mel was on oxygen and not always able to make the three-hour car trip to Chicago, so Joe often came by himself. Mary took full advantage of that time with her dad, pumping him with questions about long-dead relatives, life on the farm, and discussing news of the day.

They had many a stimulating conversation about politics, for they were on opposite sides of the fence, Joe being a lifelong Democrat, and Mary the conservative Republican. We always laughed about how we two became so conservative after both being brought up in Democratic households. I

joked that living in Chicago during the Richard J. Daley era was not con-
ducive to being Conservative…you couldn't get a garbage can in the city if
you weren't a registered Democrat! During a spirited debate with a liberal
friend, I was once asked what changed me. My response was simple, "I got
a job and started paying taxes; that's all it took."

Mary's harvested stem cells were frozen and stored in advance of the
transplant, which was scheduled for April of 1993. Unfortunately, pre-
transplant tests, specifically a MUGA scan, detected a low ejection frac-
tion, the measure of blood volume expelled by the heart when it contracts.
A normal heart ejects approximately 50 percent of its volume with each
heartbeat, but Mary's came in at around 29 percent. Dr. Rose sent us to a
cardiologist for a consult and it was a sobering experience for us. The meeting was a huge disappointment for us because the now-nameless doctor
told us that Mary could not have the transplant because the high dose chemotherapy would make her a cardiac cripple. We left that meeting feeling
pretty low, but we were not deterred. We went back to Dr. Rose and told
her that we could not accept his opinion because of the way Mary felt, and
the quality of her life. Rose agreed and decided that we should see the head
of the cardiology department at Michael Reese, Dr. Leib.

Dr. Leib was a kind and compassionate healer who immediately read
our strong will to fight and keep Mary alive. I think he quickly picked up
on how much love we felt for each other. He arranged an echo stress test
of Mary's heart so he could make his own assessment. He felt it would be
a much more accurate measure of the heart's efficiency than just a MUGA
scan. We arrived for the test with anticipation, some dread, but hopeful
for a good result. As Mary walked on the treadmill and the technician performed the echo, Dr. Leib watched the echo screen intently as he observed
Mary's level of exertion. After the test was completed, Dr. Leib told us that
Mary's heart was stronger than originally suspected, that is was a good
heart, and it could be strengthened with medication. We later learned that
Mary's septum, the wall between the ventricles, was sluggish because the
Adriamycin she received during the CHOP therapy damaged it. It is con-
sidered very cardio toxic, but again, risk and reward are to be considered.
In those days, CHOP was the most effective drug cocktail for fighting lym-
phoma, but the side effects were harsh and made life miserable for a time.

The transplant was postponed until November to give the medication
time to take effect and strengthen Mary's heart, so there was only one thing

we could do…we went back to Paris! We flew across the Atlantic—me with guidebooks, passports, and traveler's checks; Mary with a triple-lumen Hickman catheter sticking out of her chest. We had a suitcase filled with hypodermic needles, saline solution, alcohol swabs, dressings, and heparin lock. Never once were our bags searched or were we detained at Customs, either here or abroad. It was a different world in 1993. We took the shuttle to the city center, then a cab to the little pension hotel we faxed our reservation to on the Left Banque. Lo and behold, in typical Parisian fashion, the arrogant front desk person never received our fax. After arguing for a short time, being the seasoned travelers that we were, we wheeled our suitcases down the street to the next hotel, and *voilà* they had a room at a reasonable rate. After flushing Mary's port and changing the dressing, we were off on foot to explore the Left Banque.

I'm not sure how she did it, but my girl never missed a beat. We walked along the Seine holding hands and looking at the artist stalls that line the boulevard. One evening we decided to walk the cobblestone streets of the district looking for a bistro. We found a charming outdoor café at the top of the hill and dined outside. As we sat there holding hands and sipping wine waiting for our dinner, we heard the sound of a concertina coming up the street. We watched as an elderly man casually strolled up the cobblestones toward us playing "La Vie en Rose" in the moonlight. We agreed that it was the most romantic thing we'd ever experienced, and it became our song. To this day, I cannot hear that song without thinking of Mary and our evening in Paris.

After a few days in Paris, and the obligatory visit to Dehillerin for a copper pot, we drove our rental car through the Loire Valley, stopping to see some of the magnificent chateaus along the way. Chenonceu and Chambord were the two most spectacular. We were on our way to Normandy to see Omaha Beach and the island city of Mont St. Michele, when we passed fields and fields of sunflowers as far as the eye could see. It was a magical sight. After a sobering visit to historic Omaha Beach, the scene of the 1944 Allied invasion, and the American cemetery where more than ten thousand GIs are buried, we drove down to Mont St. Michele and stayed in a charming farmhouse B & B. The delightful French family made us feel very welcome and enjoyed talking to us about life in the USA. It was quite unlike the arrogant Parisians who dislike Americans, and just about everyone else.

There is now a raised causeway leading out to Mont St. Michele, unaffected by the rising tides that surround the island. We timed our visit so we could see the tides return and climbed to the very top of the mountain to see the cathedral that sits there. Mary, the cancer patient with the Hickman catheter in her chest and a damaged heart, had no trouble climbing to the top with me. We would stop and rest along the way, but there was never any question that she would make it. She wasn't about to sit alone while I made the trek. Call it bravery, stamina, determination…whatever it was made Mary who she was. Before we knew it, the sun had gone down and the tide returned. We stood near the top of Mont St. Michele looking at the moonlight shimmering on the water of the bay, holding each other, and saying how lucky we were to be there. Only Mary and I could be fighting a life-threatening disease and speak of luck. There again was a good example of our approach to the lousy hand we were dealt. The black cloud that hovered over our heads was there to keep us motivated, not to deter us.

When we arrived back in Chicago Mary spiked a fever and it was determined that, despite my best efforts, her port had become infected. It was decided that it should be removed and a new Porta Cath be put in its place. A Porta Cath is a semi-permanent access port that is implanted beneath the skin and accessed using an L-shaped Huber needle. It was far more reliable and far less prone to infection. The transplant was schedule for November, and years later Rose confided in us that she was advised by her colleagues at Hutchinson and University of Nebraska Cancer Centers, not to touch Mary with the proverbial ten-foot pole because of her heart damage. She told us that she changed her mind when we returned and told her how Mary hiked up to the top of Mont St. Michele. That convinced her that Mary was strong enough to endure the transplant, so we moved forward from that point. Nothing prepared us for what we were about to experience.

18

Creamed Corn

THE BONE MARROW TRANSPLANT

November arrived and Mary made preparations to enter the hospital by designating one of our supervisors to run The Maids in her absence. Mary was admitted to Michael Reese's Bone Marrow Transplant Unit in mid-November weighing in at 180 pounds, much to her chagrin, after months of prednisone to fight the lymphoma. Prednisone is a miracle drug that kills lymphoma but has terrible side effects, such as, weight gain, bone deterioration, sleeplessness, agitation, and steroid psychosis. Mary suffered some long-term side effects but our immediate concern was the lymphoma. The initial preparation treatment for the transplant was high-dose chemotherapy with Cytoxan, followed by total body irradiation. Mary was in a single room that was specially designed for transplantation with HEPA filtration and a double door with an inner vestibule that housed a sink for hand washing prior to entering the room in gown, gloves, and a face mask. Because of my symbiotic relationship with Mary, I was only required to wear gloves in the room.

There were other transplant patients on the floor and every time one of them was receiving his or her stem cells, the hallway reeked of the preservative used to keep the stem cells viable while frozen. It smelled like creamed corn in a can. If you open a can of creamed corn, you'll know what stem cells smell like when thawed. That smell evokes powerful memories for me. The first round of treatment was the total body irradiation. Mary partook in a number of simulations to determine the amount of material needed to evenly distribute the radiation beam. The procedure took place in a special chamber that housed a large Plexiglas casket and the radiation machine. Mary was to lie down inside the box while her body was packed in plastic bags filled with uncooked rice. Yes, rice. I immediately inquired why such a high tech procedure relied on rice! The technicians explained that because most of the body's bulk is located in the torso, the extremities absorb radiation at a faster rate and risk overexposure. It turns out that uncooked rice absorbs radiation at the same rate of body tissue, therefore, the extremities, packed in rice, do not get overexposed. Over the course of three days, Mary received 1,200 RADS of radiation, a lethal dose larger than the victims of Chernobyl were exposed to, and enough to destroy the bone marrow and kill the patient. Each of the two daily treatments were 200 RADS.

I accompanied Mary down to the radiation lab and stayed with her while they set her up for her first treatment. Each of the numbered plastic bags was strategically placed in the box and around Mary by the technician. All the time, someone in the control room was speaking to the tech over an intercom. The time came to begin the initial set up X-rays, so I was asked to leave and escorted to the control room. Mary was squeezing my hand so hard I nearly had to pry her fingers loose. She was crying and I could see the fear on her face, which was etched in my memory. She was terrified and I was powerless to take that fear away from her. It broke my heart to see her that way and all I could do was reassure her that it was what we needed to do. I went into the control room and watched as they did the preliminary testing. Again, they were speaking to each other so I knew they had the capability of communicating with Mary, but they never said a word to her. I thought that odd. After a time I was asked to wait in the waiting room for the forty minutes it would take.

Forty minutes passed, then forty-five, then fifty, and suddenly it was an hour. I got up and walked to the door of the control room, stuck my toes about one inch over the threshold, and poked my head in asking, "Is

Mary finished with the procedure?" The nurse at the controls jumped up and ran over to me saying, "You're not supposed to be in here...if the doctor sees you he won't like it!" The anger began at my toes and welled up inside me like hot magma in a volcano...then I blew my stack. I screamed at that nurse, "I don't give a fuck what your boss says...that's my wife in there and she was crying when I left her. I don't give a shit about your rules, I want to know what's going on with my wife!" I was trembling and screaming at her so loudly the doctor heard me and came running in from a side office. The nurse backed away from me and he got between us saying, "Now, Mr. DiViggiano, you can't be in there with her, you'd get irradiated!" The condescension in his voice infuriated me. I shot back, "Do you think I'm an idiot...that I don't know that? All I want is to know how Mary is doing." I continued, "You people act as though there's no human being in that chamber...you don't speak to her, reassure her, or play music to drown out the humming of that goddamned machine. She's terrified and you can't see that?" Then, as tears ran down my cheeks, I exclaimed, "She loves classical music!" The doctor was contrite and apologized profusely saying that they get so caught up in the technical nature of the treatment, sometimes they forget that they're treating a human being who has feelings.

That afternoon, after her second treatment, as Mary was being wheeled out on the gurney, she looked up at me smiling and said, "It was beautiful, they played Mozart." She went on to tell me that they talked to her about every ten minutes to tell her she was doing great and coming right along. She said that made all the difference in the world and made it far less intimidating. The subsequent treatments were almost pleasant...almost. I was empowered after that. I was not only her loving husband, I was her advocate, her enforcer, her pit bull. I could do more than just hold her hand and wipe away her tears...I could make something happen. I had never been that angry, and it felt good. It felt as though I was doing something. I was no longer helpless.

Luckily, I never again had to take that approach, and when I relayed what happened to Drs. Rose and Telfer, they assured me that it wouldn't happen to anyone else either, and I believed them. They'd never seen a patient like Mary or a husband like me. Sadly, they often saw the opposite, a husband who can't take it, who leaves a sick wife, or simply doesn't accompany her to appointments, treatments, or come to the hospital. Shame on them! No one should have to fight that battle alone. No one. Especially someone you profess to love.

The radiation made Mary very weak. It was followed by several infusions of Cytoxan in such a high dose that she reached her nadir point in about a week. The nadir is the point at which a person has no immune system—the white blood cell count drops to such a low level that simple infection can kill. It was at this point that I reached my breaking point. I was sitting in her room, in isolation, looking at her as she slept after taking an Ativan to calm her anxiousness, and I realized that my love would die if they did not have her stem cells to rebuild her immune system. That realization hit me hard. I was alone, with no one to comfort me. I went out to the hallway pay phone, pulled out my calling card, and dialed Linda Marie in Poulsbo, Washington. Linda, Mary's kindergarten best friend, is a nurse practitioner and a dear friend. I called her sobbing that I was all alone and scared. I had no one there with me and I was terrified that she would die. She did her best to reassure me that, that wasn't going to happen and asked where Mary's sisters were. I told her they were back in Iowa checking my voice mail every day for my daily update. She calmed me down and told me not to worry. I hung up, not knowing that she was already on the phone to Iowa, reading the riot act to my sisters-in-law for not being in Chicago to support me. In their defense, everyone knew Mary was in isolation and they were all terrified, my family included, that they would transmit some bug to her and make her sick.

Phyllis and Jane both came out to be with us, Phyllis first, then Jane. Having them there with us was a lifesaver for me. They provided companionship for me when Mary was uncommunicative, and they gave her the love that only a sister can give. She beamed whenever she'd open her eyes and see one of them. Mary always told the story of how different her sisters were in their approach to caring for her. Phyllis was the nurturer, the mother hen who would sit there and rub Mary's arm, sing to her, and bring her whatever she needed. Janie, on the other hand, was the take charge, medical professional, who did not cut Mary much slack. There was to be no lying in bed, she was to get up and on that exercise bike or take a walk down the hall with mask, gown, and gloves. When Mary spoke about her sisters, you could see the love in her eyes.

Her stem cells were transfused back into her on November 20, 1993, her mom's birthday. Her white cell count began to rise, helped by daily injections of Neupogen®, a drug classified as a "colony-stimulating factor" which kicks the bone marrow into high gear. Imagine this, Mary's stem cells were thawed out and infused back into her, then they magically found their way to the bone marrow and implanted. Eventually, they developed into red, white, and platelet cells to begin their new roles of transporting oxygen, killing invading bacteria, or clotting the blood in a wound. It is truly a miracle of nature and it begs the question, how do they know where to go? I can't explain it. All I know is they found their way and over time, slowly rebuilt the immune system that was wiped out by the chemotherapy and radiation.

19

So Long, Joe

YOU CAN'T BURY A CHILD

We lost Mary's mom, Amelia, in early1993 after a brief hospitalization. At eighty-three, suffering from COPD and emphysema, Mel drifted away peacefully, leaving Joe to fend for himself. Mary was between chemotherapy treatments in advance of her bone marrow transplant, but that would not deter her from being at her mom's bedside. Mary was always able to marshal some amazing reserves of energy when she was faced with an important task. There was no wringing of the hands and feeling sorry for herself. She forged ahead, stopped to throw up if need be, but continued with the task at hand, refusing to let her disease get in the way of living. In this case, in the way of helping her mom make the transition from life to death. Mary took her mom's death very hard. It doesn't matter how old you are…it's never easy saying good-bye to a parent. Amelia put the fire in Mary's belly to succeed at whatever she put her mind to, instilled the importance of a college education, taught her how to sew, and set a fine example for Mary and her sisters.

Joe took particularly good care of Amelia in her later years, tending to her every need as they sat and watched the Chicago Cubs on TV in their matching recliners. Mel was a rabid Cubs fan, as was Joe, so you can imagine their chagrin when Mary introduced them to me, a Southside Chicago White Sox fan. Horrors! We had fun teasing each other when either the Cubs or Sox were in a losing streak. It was all in good fun, and in some way, it endeared me to them.

Joe adjusted to life without Mel, played golf nearly every day in spring, summer, and fall, and frequently went to the Hy-Vee supermarket for the breakfast special. The girls always laughed because it was so hard to cook at Joe's house. He had salt and pepper, sugar, corn flakes, milk, and coffee on hand. You were on your own for the rest. Joe was close to his brother John and John's wife, Mag, so they saw each other a few times a week. Jane lived in the house behind Joe's, so she and the kids helped fend off his loneliness. He frequently drove up to Chicago to be with Mary during her apheresis, and that gave him some purpose. Joe would sit for hours, retelling stories of his childhood and running the farm. Mary could listen to those same stories over and over again. And that helped pass the time as they harvested her stem cells for the autologous peripheral stem cell rescue she was scheduled to have in the spring of 1993.

Joe Kasper was always interested in his Czech heritage, and enjoyed visits to the Czech Village and Museum in Cedar Rapids, Iowa. There is a large Czech population in the Cedar Rapids area, and many are unaware that the famous Czech composer Antonin Dvorak wrote his famous *New World Symphony* in the little town of Spillville, Iowa. Mary always thought it would be fun to take Joe to the "Old Country," and I was always interested in seeing Prague, so we discussed a trip with Joe, and he was all for it. Mary put on her travel agent cap and started planning a trip for the three of us. If memory serves, we planned a trip to Prague for the spring of 1996. We had all the plans made, tickets in hand, and the excitement in Joe made us happy. Joe Kasper's greatest fear was not that he might die, but that he might be preceded in death by one of his beloved daughters. He was committed, as was I, to keeping Mary alive and not letting her jump "out of turn."

Joe began having stomach problems in the winter of 1995, and after being treated with various antacids, his doctor decided that he should have an MRI to rule out something more sinister. Dr. Dobyns, the Kasper family doctor, dreaded having to tell Joe that he was the victim of advanced pancreatic cancer, for which the survival rate was very low. They discussed chemotherapy and the Whipple procedure, a radical surgery that resects the bowel and, at best, can prolong life for a short time. The pain and discomfort of the surgery, coupled with supportive chemotherapy, does not do much for the quality of life during that additional time. For Joe, it was an easy decision. He chose to eschew any therapy, and live out what time he had at home and with his girls. He tried to be brave about dying, made all the arrangements, got his ducks in a row, but at Christmas that year, he made a remark about a gift that he would not get to use. We all tried to play down his comment, but for the first time, I think we all heard the fear in his voice.

When Joe's condition deteriorated, we cancelled our trip to Prague, and the girls decided that they wanted to keep him in his house as long as possible, so they made a call to Iowa City Hospice. He wasn't crazy about the idea of a hospital bed in the living room, but it was really the only logical place in their small ranch home. Hospice came during the day to tend to Joe's needs, and the sisters were there at night to take care of their dad. Mary went to Iowa during the last weeks, and I joined her when it looked like Joe was getting close to leaving us. Carolyn flew in from Norway to see Joe before he died, and that made him very happy. Unfortunately, she could not stay so she missed his passing.

I remember the day vividly. It was late in the evening, and Mary was very tired, so I made her go to the back bedroom while I stayed with Joe, holding his hand. Uncle John, Aunt Mag, and Janie were all there when his breathing became very labored. I sat there holding his hand and talking to him when he took his last breath. Joe C. Kasper joined his beloved Amelia on that cold January day. Mary was devastated over losing her dad. She choked back tears as she kissed him good-bye and said, "Good job, Joe...now we don't have to worry about me jumping out of line. I love you, Daddy!"

We buried Joe that week and headed back to Chicago to continue Mary's treatment. The girls worked on going through Joe's things and preparing the remainder for a public auction in the spring. I remember being there and seeing everything neatly arranged in trays in advance of the auction, and how sick Mary was. Her red and white cell counts had dropped dangerously low, and she was in dire need of a blood transfusion, but she could not stand the thought of not being there to help finalize Joe's estate…as though the sisters would hold it against her. I assured Mary that Phyllis and Jane had things well in hand, but she insisted on being there to be a part of it all. We left Iowa on Sunday afternoon, and on Monday, Mary was back in Michael Reese Hospital with a fever and IV antibiotics hooked up to her port.

20

A Failure to Proceed

JOHN GETS A MISTRESS

In the spring of 1995, I happened to be out on sales calls in the upscale western suburb of Hinsdale, when something caught my eye. I am a self-proclaimed gear head who loves cars. One of my childhood fantasies was to own a Rolls-Royce, because I have been fascinated by this automobile for as long as I can remember. I was driving past the Rolls-Royce and Bentley dealership on Ogden Avenue when I spotted a white, 1979 Rolls-Royce Silver Shadow II on their used car lot. It was pure white, and its classic grill and "Flying Lady" hood ornament glistened in the sunlight of that beautiful spring day. It was marked "Special" and it had a price tag of $27,000. I stopped for a look and took it for a test drive. I was in heaven…I kept pinching myself for I could not believe that I was driving a Rolls-Royce down Interstate 294. The salesman was going on and on about how the cars take three months to build, and other Rolls-Royce trivia. I was oblivious because I was driving my dream car! I came home and told Mary about it. She promptly replied, "Oh, piffle…it's just a car." "Just a car? Is Royal Doulton just china?" I retorted. I had to use an example she could appreciate. Keep in mind, until I met Mary, she drove a brown 1984 Toyota Corolla, with vinyl seats, stick shift, AM radio, and no carpeting. Yes, a basic, boring, rice burner! To her, a car was a means to get from point A to point B. To her, there was no measure of prestige in a car! A big house, diamonds, emeralds, yes, but a car, no!

She was a tough cookie; I had to do some fancy convincing. I spent two days formulating my attack. I came up with a livery service adjunct to our maid service business. I crunched numbers, did research, used weddings as a good example of demand for a Rolls-Royce, and basically acted like a child who wanted something so badly, he would agree to keep his room clean for the rest of his life. For days she put me through hell. Finally, one evening after dinner, she came up to me in our family room, put her arms around me, kissed me sweetly and said, "Honey, you love that car, don't you? Anyone who wants something that badly should have it." "Really, really, are you sure?" I replied. "Oh, my God, thank you, thank you, thank you!" I yelled as I picked her up and twirled her around the room.

I took her to the dealership the next day to show her the Rolls, took her for a ride, and asked her what she thought. You could tell how disinterested she was in what she considered "just a car," then she said, "It's nice." "Nice? Just nice?" I just rolled my eyes and started the negotiations. The salesman was not interested in making a deal, but then again, he'd never before met Mary DiViggiano. You should have seen it. It was textbook Mary. "Lonnie," she said, "This is a sixteen-year-old vehicle that you are not willing to warranty. Now, admit it; it's going to take at least two thousand dollars to get this car up to John's standards," she said. Then she went for the jugular. "Lonnie, not to mention the fact that this car has been sitting on your lot for a year," she said as she raised an eyebrow. You could see him squirming in his seat. He did the old "Let me speak to my manager" bit and left the desk. I leaned over to Mary and whispered, "How do you know that?" With a wry smile on her face, she handed me a brochure, dated a year earlier, with a photo of the dealership and its line of used cars in front. Low and behold, there sat a white 1979 Rolls-Royce in the forefront marked "Special." The salesman returned and admitted that the car was the same in the photo, but since had a transmission rebuild to make it saleable, and had the service record to prove it. We went back and forth and finally settled on a price just a hair over $25,000.

I picked the Rolls up a couple of days later after they fixed a few things that needed repair, and promptly joined the Lake Michigan Region

Rolls-Royce Owners Club. We frequently attended club functions and met some great people, some of whom are still good friends. Mind you, there are two types of Rolls owners: simple, down-to-earth folks, many with a great deal of money who truly love the marquee, and the wealthy, pretentious, pompous types, who only love themselves and the attention their cars garner for them. We had little to do with those types, who I found to be so full of themselves and arrogant. They were not worth our time.

Mary would just roll her eyes when I'd mention another club function, but she dutifully went along, and I think she had a really nice time. She was the practical daughter of Amelia Kasper, so she was philosophically opposed to buying that car, but she loved me dearly, and when she saw how much I wanted it, she couldn't say no any longer. I loved her for that. Mary used to say the Rolls was my mistress, "I know that if he's not with me, he's out in the garage with that car." The car was my mistress, but it became the proverbial money pit over the next six years. It had a number of breakdowns, aka "failures to proceed" as R-R refers to them, but despite the expense, I had more fun with that car, and my girl looked spectacular riding in it.

The car was my pride and joy, and it made me feel like a million bucks to drive it. People would crane their necks to see who was driving that magnificent car. Little did they know that I was just a hard working Chicago southsider who happened to be a car nut, and loved the elegant English automobiles.

———

Mary and I were opera lovers, and we maintained a season subscription to the Chicago Lyric Opera. On special winter evenings, weather permitting, we would drive downtown in the Rolls, me in my tuxedo, and Mary in her full-length ranch mink coat, and arrive regally at the Lyric Opera House. We'd give the car to the valet and make our entrance, all eyes upon us, wondering who we were. It was great fun. I particularly enjoyed driving the car through a McDonald's drive thru. Invariably, the kid at the window would ask, "Is that a Bentley?" or "Is that a Mercedes?" Not once did anyone guess correctly...much to my consternation!

Later, after we hit the road in our motor home, I stored the Rolls in Iowa, and we'd drive it when we visited in the summertime. When I decided that sitting for months was not good for the car, I had it shipped down to Palm Springs. I drove it down here for several months, then, after having $1,700 in brake work done, I decided to put the car on consignment with a local exotic car dealer. It was like giving a child up for adoption. When we dropped off the car at the dealership, the salesman asked if we wanted to be driven back home in the Rolls. I replied, "No, take the keys...I don't want to see the car again!" I couldn't bear the thought of being driven back in it. We drove back in a Chevy.

No other car before it or since has held such a fascination for me. I had "arrived", and my childhood dream had come true. It was a wonderful six-year love affair.

21

Happy Birthday, Mom

THE MAJORETTE

My mom, Helen, turned eighty on December 27, 1997. This proud Polish woman never sought help unless she was absolutely unable to do something herself. She lived alone after my dad passed away on April 30, 1990, of a massive heart attack. I suppose the years of Dad's doing his own thing prepared Mom for being alone, but she would never admit that. There was never any indication when we were kids that my mom and dad weren't happy together, but somehow I can't imagine his sitting in a tavern every weekend evening was something she cared for.

Mom was cleaning her kitchen one day and decided to climb up onto the kitchen counter to clean the greenhouse window over the sink. She lost her balance, fell, and broke her shoulder, but she called my sister Jean who promptly got her treatment. The orthopedic doctor put Mom on a regimen of painkillers and anti-inflammatory medications while she healed. Unfortunately, the drug combination she was taking caused her stomach distress, but she didn't say anything until the damage was done. I advised her to stop taking the painkiller if it hurt her stomach. She stopped taking it, but it was too late. The pain must have been too much for her so she started taking the painkillers again.

One day, my sister Cathy came home from her day program at Thresholds, and walked into the bathroom, which was a bloody mess. She called out for Mom who answered in a very weak voice. There she was, lying in her bed covered with blood. Cathy's first inclination was to call my sister Jean who lived across the alley. Jean ran over and immediately called 911. Mom explained that she felt the urge to move her bowels but didn't make it to the toilet in time. She lost control and expelled all the blood that was filling her bowels due to the ruptured artery in her stomach. She tried to get up, but lost her balance and fell onto the bathtub, breaking a couple of ribs. She was in a great deal of pain as she dragged herself to the bedroom. There was a phone in the bathroom, but she didn't have the presence of mind to call someone. We have no idea how long she laid there before my sister returned home.

The paramedics immediately started an IV, and even though Mom was able to speak, they could not find a pulse. She was taken to the ER and started on blood products and fluids. Mary and I raced to the hospital to find her stabilized and speaking. The ER team did an endoscopy and saw the artery pulsing blood into her stomach, so they immediately cauterized it through the endoscope. We stayed with her until late in the evening, and Mary remarked that her biggest regret was not staying overnight with Mom, for she could sense the fear in her voice. The doctors said that the cauterization may or may not hold, and that they tend to re-bleed after eating solid food. The consensus was that if it were to re-bleed, they'd want it to do so in the hospital.

She was admitted to the hospital and given medication to control the pain of the two broken ribs she sustained when she fell against the bathtub. They gave Mom solid food for lunch the next day and her ulcer began to bleed, just as they feared. The hospital called to tell us that they had to do emergency surgery to stop the bleeding. I ran down to the hospital immediately and found them wheeling Mom into surgery. My sister Cathy accompanied me, so we were both there with her in pre-op to reassure her that everything was going to be okay, and to tell her that we loved her. That was the last time I was able to speak to my mom.

The surgery was a success, but Mom never came out of the anesthesia; she may have suffered a stroke during surgery. She remained on the ventilator for nearly three weeks, and when her major organs began to shut down we were faced with a heart-wrenching decision. Mom had an advance directive, or living will, and I was her medical power of attorney. So after consulting with a neurologist and with input from her physician, it was decided that even if by some miracle, Mom was to come out of the coma, her quality of life would be very poor. Mary was at Mom's bedside every day.

During of our vigil on May 5, Mary turned fifty years old. Since we weren't much in the mood to celebrate, I gave Mary a choice: dinner in the hospital cafeteria, or at the Majorette Restaurant, which was kitty-corner from the hospital, right across the Burlington Railroad tracks in Berwyn. She opted for the Majorette. Mary spoke of how much she loved and admired my mother, a woman who had to raise herself because her own mother was mentally ill. She was a kind and loving mother-in-law who never tried to give Mary unsolicited advice. Mary always called my mom Helen and loved to hear her tell stories about my childhood. Her favorite was when my brother or I failed to take out the trash. It had a habit of showing up on our beds! Mom had a way of making her point...thank God Mary didn't follow her lead.

We had Mom removed from life support on May 15, 1998, and she passed away quietly after only a minute or so.

She was the last of our four parents to leave this Earth, and her passing became the catalyst for our next great adventure.

22

Out Of Our Minds

THE DIPLOMAT

We made the preparations for Mom's funeral and went home exhausted after our three-week daily vigil at her bedside. We were lying in our hammock on May 17, our anniversary, holding each other and talking about life. We discussed my mom's passing and how we had lost all four of our parents, Mary's continued health issues, and the stress related to having a business. We also agreed that we had a big, beautiful home with a big mortgage payment, and we hardly had time to enjoy it. We were never quite sure who came up with it first, but eventually we hit upon the idea of traveling around the country in a motor home. It was my dad's dream to have a motor home and go wherever his whim dictated. I recalled looking at motor homes in the mid-1970s with him, but he could never convince my mom to do it.

In our case, the stock market was booming at the time, so we did some quick number crunching in our heads and decided that we could afford to sell everything and hit the road until retirement age. Our IRAs were doing well and we could live off the sale of the house and the business.

We realized that the business could take several years to sell, so there was never any immediacy to our dream. Mary had relapsed from the bone marrow transplant and was undergoing another round of chemotherapy, and she knew that there were no guarantees in life, so we made our decision, and put the business up for sale. We registered with a business broker the next day.

I can be the impetuous type when it comes to things on wheels, so we went to look at motor homes, just to see what was out there and at what price. Mind you, I'm not a shopper, I'm a buyer—if I find something I like and I feel it's a good value, I'll buy it. When Mary first moved to Chicago, we decided we needed a new barbeque grill, and so it started. Mary and I went out looking for a new grill, and we saw one that I really liked for a reasonable price. But no, Mary felt compelled to drive to a number of stores and compare models and prices. That was an exercise in futility, because as you can probably guess, we went right back and bought the very first grill we looked at. So much for comparison shopping. Mary would repeat that ritual a number of times throughout our marriage.

Despite my impetuous nature, I do like to do some research before diving into something, so we visited some nearby RV dealerships to see what we might like to live in full time. The dealers nearby sold mostly travel trailers and small RVs. The upscale coaches were at dealerships in the far northwestern suburbs of Chicago. After looking at some low-line Class A coaches, we decided that they weren't deluxe enough to be someone's full-time home. They were fine if you're just spending a weekend in it, but lacking some of the amenities we'd become accustomed to.

Annie and Daniel, the two farm kids, were visiting us one weekend, so we decided to take a ride and look at some high-line coaches on Saturday. Naturally, the salesman started us out in a $400,000 motor home that looked like a palace on wheels, but then reality set in, and we agreed that we had to set our sights much lower. I made up my mind early that we would not buy a new coach anyway. I'd let the first buyer take the big depreciation hit. I asked to see some pre-owned coaches in our price range, and there just so happened to be a recent trade-in that the salesman thought we might like. The coach had just arrived from its maiden voyage to and from Florida with an owner who decided he'd rather have a $400,000 coach instead. The thirty-eight-foot 1998 Monaco Diplomat had about 3,000 miles on it and the bugs were still on the windshield. (I later found out that it had

plenty of other "bugs," but that's a book in itself.) We test drove the beast with Annie, Daniel, and our cocker spaniel, Lady. We all agreed that it was indeed livable, and the price was right. So after convincing Mary that we had to jump on this one, we started negotiating.

Mary DiViggiano is the kind of person you want on your side of the desk when there's negotiating to be done. I swear that in a former life she spent time in an Arabian bazaar because she could sell sand in the desert! We not only negotiated the price to where we wanted it to be, but we got them to throw in a front mask to protect the paint, a tow dolly so we could bring along our Cadillac, and six months of free storage since we had yet to sell the house. They washed the bugs off the coach and we took delivery that day. Since we were going to drop the kids off at a halfway point on Sunday anyway, we decided to drive our new home out to the farm in Iowa and surprise the family. We pulled out of the dealership in our new motor home and I took to driving it as if I'd driven one all my life. Mary would later learn to drive it and did quite well, particularly on the interstates. She wasn't too keen on driving it in town, but she could if she had to. That girl knew no fear long before it became a corporate catch phrase.

I drove the coach onto Interstate 88 and pointed it west toward Iowa. It handled beautifully, and the kids were having a great time playing with the dog and watching TV as we rolled down the highway. The tranquility of the moment changed as we approached the first toll both on I-88. All was fine until I hit the first "rumble strips" at about fifty miles per hour. Rumble strips are placed on the pavement to warn you to slow down for the upcoming tollbooth. Lady, our cocker spaniel, was very good in the car and seemed to be equally as comfortable in the motor home, until I hit the rumble strips. She immediately ran up front looking for me and inter-twined her body in my legs, blocking access to the brake pedal. Luckily, I had my foot off the accelerator and had the presence of mind to switch on the engine brake to help slow the motor home. Mary managed to get Lady out from under my feet in time for me to stop at the toll booth. I opened the window and looked down at the young lady toll attendant, and with a face as white as a sheet, said in a quivery voice, "It's my first toll in my brand new motor home...how much do I owe you?" I was so shaken by the dog incident that I must have sounded like a nervous Nellie. She just looked up at me and smiled, then said, "Your first toll in your brand new motor home? Go ahead, no charge!" She probably saw the fear on my face.

Mary and I looked at each other and burst out in laughter. That was just the first of many crazy things to happen in that coach.

We dropped the kids off at the farm and showed Mary's family what we were going to live in after we sold the house. They told us later that they thought we had lost our minds. We drove back to Chicago, put the motor home in storage, and got busy trying to sell the business, which did not take us very long.

On occasion, we decided to take the motor home out for a weekend of camping, just to get used to living full time on the road. On one particular occasion, we got the Diplomat out of storage and drove it out to a campground in Galesburg, Illinois. As I guided the coach down Interstate 80, I kept scanning the gauges to make sure everything was running as it should. As we approached the Ottawa, Illinois, area, I happened to look down at the transmission as I planned to downshift in anticipation of a grade, and noticed that the LED indicator that displays the gear you are driving in was blank! And the buttons to change gears were inoperative. And did I mention that I was running low on diesel fuel? Yes, I had to stop for fuel and now I wasn't sure I could get the transmission back into gear if I shut the engine down to refuel. Murphy's Law is alive and well when you live in a motor home.

I exited the interstate and drove into a truck stop, then pulled the coach up to the diesel pumps, keeping my foot on the brake with the engine running. I had Mary go out and tell the attendant that I was unable to pump the gas because we could not turn off the engine! To this day, I wonder what she said to that guy! She came back with a greasy good ol' boy, with the biggest grin on her face, giggling and joking with him. I'm sure she made up some story about her white-collar husband who had no idea of what he's doing...even though she knew better.

We fueled her up, and were back on the road in short order. As I drove down the highway, I would glance down to see if there was any life in the transmission selector. Lo and behold, I hit a bump in the road, and noticed that the LEDs were lit up again! A loose electrical connection...but where? The transmission remained lit up and the gear selection feature worked just fine—that is, until we got on the back road that led to the campground. I hit a pothole and the transmission selector went dark again!

At this point, we needed to stop at the front office to register and find out what campsite they had reserved for us. Once again, I stayed in

the coach with the engine running, foot on the brake, while Mary went inside and told them our sob story. I felt bad sitting there, while our diesel exhaust fumes ruined the evening for the campers nearby. In the interest of being a thoughtful camper, I shut the engine down.

I was amazed to see a crowd gathering around the motor home, as I nosed around in the compartment that housed the fuses. Everyone wanted to know if I had trouble with my rig. When I said that I had an electrical problem, the recommendations began to fly from every male in the group. I traced down fuses, only to find them all in good condition, and the job was getting increasingly more difficult as the sun began to go down. Luckily, someone came over with a powerful flashlight. I then identified a large wire loom that led to a gray plastic plug, and it was labeled "transmission". The fact that it was an intermittent problem, and often associated with going over a bump in the road, I decided to pull out the plug and see if the male end was seating properly into the female end.

When I separated the two plug ends, and with the flashlight shining inside the female plug, I could see a small blob of soundproofing that must have fallen into the open plug during the construction process. I carefully removed it and reseated the plug. Problem solved!

23

The Talking House

MOVING FORWARD

The Maids business sold in October of 1998, so we found ourselves in a predicament because our means of income was gone and the mortgage payments were still due. It was clear that we should have sold the house first. We had a neighbor across the street that was a Realtor, and she offered to give us an appraisal, hoping we would list the house with her. We decided not to list with her for two reasons. We weren't happy with the listing price she suggested, and her commission would have eaten up a chunk of the money we intended to live on until we were able to start drawing on our IRA and 401K retirement funds. I did some research and found an Internet company that helped you sell your house on your own. They provided a sign and a listing on the MLS, all for a flat fee of about $1,000. Another friend of mine was a Realtor in the city who was interested in developing a sell-it-yourself program, so he was interested in the process and offered to help me by loaning me a Talking House machine. It was a radio transmitter that broadcasts a prerecorded message on a specific frequency. A sign was placed in front of the house inviting interested parties to dial their radio to hear a continuously looping message about the home. It was unique and very effective.

A young, engaged to be married couple, looked at the house a couple of times and submitted an offer. The offer was so low, I found it insulting, but Mary kept her cool and told me to make a counter offer. I countered for a few thousand less and they came back a few thousand higher. We continued this exercise until we settled on a figure, which happened to be the listing price our neighbor suggested. We sold our house for about $1,000 in expenses and paid no commission.

Since we were moving into our motor home we had to sell off most of our things, so we planned the "We're Not Dead Yet Estate Sale". We decided to put a price tag on everything in the house and were prepared to bargain if need be. To our surprise, we discovered that if you call it an "Estate Sale" you are able to charge anything you want and get it, but if you call it a "Garage" or "Yard" sale, you're lucky to get fifty cents. The sale was planned for a Saturday and Sunday, and was limited to friends, family, and neighbors. You can imagine my surprise when I answered the front door bell to find a rather large, middle-aged woman with five small children in tow. I asked if I could help her, and she held up the flier that I put in my neighbor's mailboxes. We had the rural-style, roadside mailboxes in our development, so, being the "rocket scientist" that I am, decided to cut out the Postal Service and just slip a flier announcing the sale into each one. How does that saying go? "The best laid plans of mice and men…" When I stuttered and stammered for a good explanation, others were arriving for the sale, so I simply invited her and her brood to come in. I asked how she happened to get my flier and she explained that she worked at the Post Office, and it was pinned to the bulletin board in the employee lounge. I mentally slapped myself in the forehead, realizing that our postal delivery person saw the illegally placed flier in one of the neighbor's boxes, and thought I needed to be taught a lesson.

It was all very harmless until the lady and her minions came to the checkout station we'd set up on our kitchen island. She laid out her "goods" and Mary's eyes nearly popped out of their sockets! She then let out an, "Oh, My God!" and scooped up the pile of costume jewelry the woman was about to purchase. She shrieked, "Where did you get this?" and the lady calmly stated that she opened the jewelry box that was sitting on the dresser in the master bedroom. To which Mary responded, "These are NOT for sale...and how dare you open my jewelry box!" (The jewelry box was marked "Not for Sale.") The lady was clearly embarrassed and apologized profusely, and Mary quickly calmed down and apologized for her outburst. No one could blame Mary because much of what the woman tried to buy was Mary's collection of expensive Swarovski crystal brooches and earrings that I'd bought for her over the years. A quick inventory showed nothing missing, so we were lucky she didn't slip anything in her pockets. It was our fault for not locking the jewelry box, or for not assigning docents to each room in the house. We never thought to do so because it was intended to be a closed sale. The lady purchased other things that had a price tag, and everyone calmed down, so there was no harm done. I must admit to cringing whenever the doorbell rang after that incident.

Nearly everything sold on Saturday, with the exception of the piano and the white living room sofa. The piano went to a dealer on consignment and the sofa sold a week later from an ad in the local paper. Our homebuyer bought $2,000 worth of furniture and the remaining items were donated to a local charity.

Mary was in the hospital when the closing took place. She was being treated for one of the many infections she was prone to because of her suppressed immune system. I took the buyers on a final walk-through of the house the day of the closing. Without our things in it, it was just an empty house, not the home we came to love.

24

Italia

THE POPE, THE GYPSY, AND THE TOURIST.

Mary had a remarkable way of bouncing back after treatment. Once she was on the mend, we decided to take a trip to Italy before hitting the road in the motor home. She went into travel agent mode and planned our itinerary, booked our flights, and made sure our passports were in order. On March 30, 1999, we flew to Rome and stayed in a central Rome bed and breakfast that Mary had prearranged. The old city was as magnificent as I remembered, but we were both taken aback at the amount of graffiti defacing Rome, more than we ever remembered seeing. It was on any flat surface—walls, billboards, garbage trucks, and ancient antiquities. It was very disappointing to see.

We walked the streets of Rome visiting the Coliseum, Roman Forum, the Vatican, Piazza Navona, Piazza di Spagna, Trevi Fountain, and the Pantheon. For a person who endured countless chemotherapy treatments, Mary had amazing stamina, and loved to walk when we were on vacation. It was Good Friday, our third and final day in Rome, so we elected to visit the Vatican before heading south. St. Peter's was probably a bit more crowded than normal because of the Catholic holy day. We mingled with the crowd as we walked through the enormous piazza in front of the basilica, which was being set up for the afternoon mass given by the pope.

Once inside, we made our way to the crypt that lies beneath the altar in St. Peter's basilica, passing Michelangelo's Pieta, and the crowds gathered in front of it. It wasn't behind Plexiglas the first time I saw it—that security measure was installed after a crazed person attacked and damaged the priceless masterpiece with a hammer a few years earlier.

The entrance to the crypt is to the left as you face the magnificent altar with its incredibly ornate canopy, the baldacchino, a Bernini masterpiece. It rises ninety-five feet above the altar, and is breathtaking. We entered the crypt down a narrow staircase and walked through the labyrinth that houses the tomb of St. Peter and a number of other popes, including Pius VI.

We exited the crypt on the opposite side of the altar to find a group of people gathered along a railing in the right transept of the basilica. It was nearly twelve noon and the cordoned-off area was guarded by men in dark suits and sunglasses, with earpieces very much like the president's Secret Service.

At exactly noon the doors opened and out came Pope John Paul II, who, even in 1999, was in failing health and hunched over. He blessed the crowd as he walked toward a large chair in the center, with a long line of people standing in line to see him. I must say that my twelve years of Catholic education made my heart do a flip-flop as the pope gave us his blessing. There was an aura about him that we both recognized, but were unable to explain. I cannot deny that we were both enveloped in a warm feeling that made us smile. By sheer coincidence we happened upon the pope's Good Friday confession, and the people waiting in line were penitents chosen to confess to the pope by special invitation. We left the Vatican and giggled after we both looked at each other and said, "Would you want to confess to the pope?"

Our next destination was Sorrento and the Amalfi Coast. We took the train to Naples and connected to another that stopped at Pompei. We spent hours exploring this archeological marvel, with its beautifully preserved frescos and mosaics, not to mention the ancient pornography, much of which is now in a museum in Naples. The most haunting sights in Pompei are the pumice shells of the victims. The bodies are long gone, but the image of the victim's final pose is perfectly preserved in volcanic ash.

It was then on to Sorrento, famous for its Limoncello, a lemon liqueur, and beautiful handmade music boxes. After a few magical days in Sorrento, a boat ride to gorgeous Capri, and a breathtaking bus ride to Amalfi along the Amalfi Coast—passing through places like picturesque Positano—we took the train back to Rome to connect to a high speed train that would take us to Venice. On the train to Venice, we encountered a problem with our assigned seats and had to elicit the help of a young Italian woman named Anna who sat beside us. Once we had the problem resolved with her help, Mary engaged in a conversation with her. She was an interesting woman who taught English at the Aviano NATO base near Venice. In the space of those few hours, Mary and I developed a friendship with this young woman that continued even after Mary's death. We keep in touch via e-mail, and she has shared pictures of her newborn son with me.

After a rainy few days in Venice, and a disappointing visit to the glass factory on Murano, we took the train to Verena on Lake Como and booked a few nights in a charming pensione overlooking the lake. Our room was on the second floor, with a delightful balcony and green shutters on either side, framing a postcard view of the town and the lake beyond.

Mary was fatigued from the long train ride, so she rested that afternoon and I gave our itinerary a modification or two. We spent two blissful days in the Italian Lake District, taking a boat ride to Bellagio and dining at one charming trattoria after another. We always said that we never had a bad meal, or a bad bottle of wine in Italy—and Lake Como was no exception.

We had a lot more to see in Italy, so we left Lake Como and took the train to the Italian Riviera, also known as the Cinque Terre (five lands). This area was not what we expected. We thought we'd see marinas filled with luxurious yachts, beautiful Sophia Loren lookalikes, and playboys driving their Ferraris. On the contrary, the town of Vernazza is one of five seaside villages built on a hillside and connected by challenging hiking trails with breathtaking views of the Ligurian Sea. We found a bed and breakfast while walking down a cobblestone street toward the harbor; it happened to be a third floor walk-up, but it was clean and cozy. Once again, Mary was running out of gas, so she had to take her time climbing up to our room.

After a short rest, we went out to explore the town. Mary had fun try-ing to turn her Spanish into Italian. Believe it or not, she was pretty good at communicating with the Italians, and they seemed to enjoy the chal-lenge. Mary always found pleasure in the simplest of things. She would laugh because the mere mention of my surname always initiated a bar-rage of Italian—they thought I *must* speak the language with a name like DiViggiano!

We walked up the hill to a tower that housed a bar with a terrace overlooking the Ligurian Sea, and watched the sunset. It was a spectacular sight. We wound up spending an extra day in Vernazza due to a rail strike, one of many that plagued us during our three weeks in Italy.

Once the trains began running, nothing ran on schedule for days. We finally booked a seat on a train to the hill towns of Assisi, Siena, Perugia, and Orvieto. Each town had its own magic: Assisi with it's beautiful cathe-dral, damaged during a recent earthquake; Perugia, known for its candy; Siena, home of the famous Palio horse race; and Orvieto, a medieval fortress town built on a huge plateau.

Siena was a favorite of ours with its steep, narrow cobblestone streets, and glorious history. We found a charming bed and breakfast that was run by nuns and near the Church of St. Catherine. She is the patron saint of Italy, and has the dubious distinction of being in two places at once. She died in 1380, and her body is entombed in Rome, but her head is in Siena at the Church of St. Catherine.

The convent was built on a hill, so you had to take an elevator down to your room. We put our things in our tiny room, complete with a Bible, a cru-cifix, and a picture of the Sacred Heart, and walked back to the elevator for the ride back up to street level. We got to the elevator and could not find the call button. We stood there puzzled and decided to knock on a nearby door after hearing children's voices. It was a day care center. The door flew open, and there stood a large nun, in full habit (very much like the Dominicans who terrorized us as kids at St. Richard's School in Chicago), flailing her arms and prattling in Italian. Mary said my eyes were again the size of saucers as I was reduced to that little boy who was caught riding his bike in the churchyard! The Sister quickly deduced our dilemma, took my room key from my hand, flashed a huge smile and put the key in a keyhole that was clearly visible (once you knew where it was). We thanked her in our best Italian, and she smiled broadly as she backed into the doorway to the screeching mass of children in her charge.

Mary could not contain herself as we rode up to street level in that tiny elevator. She said, "You should have seen the look on your face when that nun came flying out of that door!" She was in tears and nearly doubled over in laughter. Only I know the fear of having a nun yelling at you and flailing her arms, and I have the psychological scars to prove it.

Our first stop was the Church of St. Catherine to visit her shrine. It was a rather simple church, by European standards, unassuming and medieval. Adjacent to the altar was a crypt with a strange metallic cap topped with a symbolic crown of thorns. That is where St. Catherine's head is entombed.

This excerpt from the book, Joan of Arc, by Francis C. Lowell (1896), about Joan of Arc and St. Catherine of Siena, will give the reader some indication of what her life was like:

Catherine was an extreme ascetic. The monk who wrote her life was undoubtedly credulous, but when ample allowance has been made for his exaggerations, there remains a true story of ingenious self-torture. As a child she flogged and starved herself. When a little older, she plunged herself into hot water. She constructed for herself a bed on which sleep must have been painful, and fastened a chain about her waist next to her skin, in order to guard against passions which in her must have been imaginary. Ordinary neatness she considered a sin, and she was in great distress because she believed herself to love her sister too much. The punishments which she inflicted on herself for shrinking from loathsome disease cannot be told, they are themselves so loathsome.

We walked around the church, looking at various spots with historical significance, stopping at a glass case filled with artifacts. They turned out to be some of St. Catherine's personal items: her prayer book, a scrap of cloth, a flagellation device with a handle and leather straps used to inflict pain during prayer, and the strangest of relics. I called Mary over and asked, "Is that what I think it is?" She looked at it, eyes wide, and said, "It's a finger!" Yes, it was St. Catherine's finger; a thin, wrinkled, nearly black appendage, complete with a fingernail, standing upright in a sort of candlestick. We were both standing there with our mouths open trying to comprehend what we were seeing.

So, the patron saint of Italy is in at least three pieces, and we speculated that this one was her middle finger. We believed she was using it to answer to her detractors…from the grave!

After a number of days exploring the wonderful Tuscan and Umbrian hill towns, we headed back to Rome to catch our flight back to the States. On our last day in Rome, we decided that we hadn't spent enough time exploring the Roman Forum, so off we went. I was wearing a fisherman's vest that I purchased in Siena, and was keeping my wallet zipped into the left front pocket. The zipper was sticking and giving me fits all morning, but that wasn't enough to save me from what was about to happen. We were walking across a bridge that lead into the Forum, and noticed a group of young gypsy girls milling about. One of them was carrying an infant, and most of them were holding cardboard signs. They spotted me wearing my black leather jacket, and immediately ran over to beg for money. Their ages ranged from as young as twelve to perhaps twenty-five, the oldest one carried the infant.

They crowded around me, ignoring Mary completely, pushing their cardboard signs at me horizontally. All this time, unbeknownst to me, one of the youngest girls was quietly, and deftly unzipping my vest pocket. I had my hands up in the air, not wanting to touch them, and was politely telling them to move away because I did not have any money (not too far from the truth after three weeks in Italy). Little did they know that Mary had most of our cash, traveler's checks, and passports in the purse she was closely clutching.

I finally pushed them aside, took a few steps beyond them, and because of my Chicago upbringing instinctively reached for my wallet, only to find that it was gone. I spun around, and charged back at them, screaming expletives at the top of my lungs like a raging bull. One youngster was standing alone, with her head down and her arm extended, holding my wallet out toward me. I ripped it from her hand and screamed loudly in her face about how I was going to turn her over to the police. She was probably in training and not savvy enough to hand it off to an accomplice or toss it over the bridge for later retrieval, and I probably scared the crap out of her. Despite that traumatic event, we enjoyed our last day at the Forum and the end of what was to be our last vacation abroad together.

25

See the USA...

JOHN AND MARY GO "FULL TIME"

We returned to Chicago and drove out to Phyllis's farm where our motor home was being stored while we were in Italy. It was late spring and we were anxious to hit the road and begin our new lifestyle. We knew that Mary's kindergarten best friend, Linda Marie, and her husband, Ken, were in West Branch visiting Linda's family, so we arranged for them to ride back to Seattle with us on our first road trip in our new abode. Ken had owned an RV, so his expertise came in handy along the way. Being a novice, I wasn't sure how some RV systems worked, and I wasn't adept at backing up and pulling into campgrounds, so Ken helped me get my "sea legs." We started out on Monday, June 7, 1999, stopped in Lincoln, Nebraska, for one night to see Mary's Aunt Lorna and Uncle Lester, and then we drove to Denver to see Ken's mom and stepdad. We spent the night parked at the curb outside Ken's folk's house, and then drove north to Yellowstone National Park, passing by Grand Teton National Park. Mary and Linda had a great time catching up while Ken and I did the driving and navigating.

Yellowstone, the first of the National Parks, designated so by Teddy Roosevelt, was as spectacular as I'd heard, and truly a national treasure. We spent a few days camping in the park, and seeing such famous sites as Old Faithful, Yellowstone Canyon and Falls, Geyser Basin, and the many hundreds of thermal features throughout the park. We then set off north through the Gallatin National Forest on our way to Interstate 90 for the trip west to Seattle.

As we drove along, we began to see signs touting "Rocky Mountain Oysters," which are actually deep-fried calf testicles, a local delicacy. There were signs near every exit; so many that the final sign was inevitable. It pronounced the "Testicle Festival" which would be held that fall. We roared with laughter, and couldn't help but wonder what that little gala would be like.

Both Ken and Linda are nurse practitioners in a small town on the Olympic Peninsula of Washington State. Little did we know that their medical expertise would come in handy on this cross-country trip. We were heading West on I-90, having just passed over the summit at Snoqualmie Pass, going downhill toward Seattle. Ken was driving and pulled into the left lane to pass a slow-moving truck. Up ahead, a small, dark blue compact car was in our lane and started to weave a bit. Ken pointed it out to us, and as soon as all eyes were trained on the car ahead, it careened into the center concrete divider, bounced off and went airborne, rolling over sideways across two lanes and into the gutter, stopped only by a tree stump sitting in the culvert. Somehow, Ken managed to get the fifteen-ton motor home and Jeep over to the right shoulder and stopped in an amazingly short amount of time. As soon as he hit the parking brake, he was out the door and racing toward the upside down vehicle. I was close behind as Mary and Linda dialed 911 on their cell phones. When we reached the car, Ken stuck his head into the driver's side window and found the young man conscious and trying to extricate himself. After determining that there was no spinal cord injury, Ken helped him crawl out of the window of the upturned car. I recall seeing CDs strewn all over the interior and exterior of the car. The young driver claimed that he had fallen asleep at the wheel, but I couldn't help but think that perhaps he dropped a CD on the floor and lost control of the car as he was reaching for it. It just seemed unlikely that such a young man would fall asleep…but I could be wrong. The paramedics arrived shortly thereafter, along with the State Police, who asked us for a statement.

Once we knew the young man was in good hands, we said good-bye, accepting his heartfelt thanks, and continued down the mountain. The smell of burning brakes was pungent as we climbed back into the motor home to relay the story to Mary and Linda.

The rest of the trip was uneventful; until we got to their house and I determined that their driveway was a bit overgrown to fit my motor home, without scratching the paint job. With their permission, I went out and proceeded to trim the offending branches—fanatic that I am!

I pulled into the drive, and parked the motor home in the grassy field adjacent to their house, where Ken had installed water, sewer, and power for just this purpose. They have a lovely expanse of grass, so our cocker spaniel, Lady, literally had a ball out there playing fetch. The only disconcerting things were the banana slugs. They are disgusting creatures that look like big yellow bananas crawling on the ground. Ken is also a bit of a "collector," so the yard was strewn with his many garage sale treasures, including a couple of boats that he'd planned to put in the water.

By the time we reached Poulsbo, Mary was suffering from pleural effusion, and was having a difficult time breathing. Pleural effusion is a common problem in lymphoma patients. The lymphatic fluid does not drain properly, and builds up in the space between the lungs and the chest cavity (the pleura). We suspected that the high altitudes exacerbated it, and we knew that we had to deal with it so Mary could breathe freely. A quick call to Dr. Rose in Chicago was all we needed. She directed Mary to begin a course of prednisone and Lasix, the latter being a powerful diuretic. A few days later she was ready to go.

The other thing about their place was the rain! It rained, more or less, for about nineteen of the twenty-one days we spent there. We were told that if you wanted to see the sun, you had to drive up to Sequim, so we said good-bye to Ken and Linda, and drove up there. Lo and behold, the sun came out! For some strange reason, the Olympic Peninsula can be socked in with rain and fog, yet the sun comes out at Sequim. It's a meteorological mystery that actually has something to do with wind currents...so I'm told.

After getting our fill of Vitamin D, we went back to see Ken and Linda again before we headed south toward the Oregon Coast.

There were some issues with our coach that needed attention, so we worked our way down to Oregon, where there is no state sales tax. We went to an RV dealer south of Portland and ordered a set of awnings for our two bedroom windows. They measured and told us it would take a couple of days to get them, so we parked in the Camping World parking lot and went up to spend a couple of nights with our friends Len and Marietta. They had a beautiful home up on the crest of a hill, overlooking the Coastal Range of Oregon.

We had a delightful time with them, catching up on all the gossip about my former employer (Marietta and I worked together for a number of years), and taking a trip through the Columbia River Gorge. That evening we had dinner with Len and Marietta at a charming restaurant in the trendy Twenty-Fourth Street District.

So there we were, on the Oregon Coast, exploring while we waited for the correct awnings to be delivered. We witnessed the rain and gloom that is so common to the Oregon Coast, punctuated by magnificent sites like Cannon Beach, and quaint towns like Newport. We enjoyed the scenery, despite the clouds, overcast skies, and rain

The awnings arrived at the dealer, and they were the wrong fabric color and size, so they reordered. At this point, we felt like the Lost Tribes of Israel, and not anxious to spend more time on the rainy Oregon coast. We instructed the dealer to ship them directly to the farm in Iowa where I would install them myself, which I later did.

———

When I look back at pictures of us during that trip, I can't help but notice that Mary was exhibiting a classic side effect of prednisone use, the round "moon face" effect. At the time, I guess I didn't really notice, but as I look back I can't help but feel for her. I'm sure she knew she looked that way, and must have felt self-conscious about it, but she never, ever complained. She was determined to be able to breathe and keep up with me on a walking tour of a city, so if she was going to have a moon face due to prednisone... so be it.

Prednisone is a miracle drug that kills lymphoma and helps manage some of the symptoms of the disease, unfortunately, it can cause damage to other organs in the process. Years later, Mary suffered severe pain in her right shoulder. X-rays and MRIs confirmed that she suffered from AVN (avascular necrosis of the shoulder), caused by years of prednisone use. At one point, she was taking 80 mg per day. The top of the humerus bone in the upper arm is rounded, designed to fit neatly into the shoulder socket. In AVN of the shoulder, the blood supply is cut off to that part of the bone due to the prednisone, so the cells become necrotic, or die. The normally rounded end of the bone flattens, and no longer fits into the shoulder socket. You can imagine the pain it would cause. Again, Mary suffered in silence because she knew that she needed the prednisone, and was determined not to let it slow her down.

Becoming an invalid because of her illness was not in the plan. She had too much living to do, and was not about to let this disease and its many debilitations get in the way. I know now that she was putting on a brave face for my benefit. Her goal was to stay by my side for as long as possible, and I think that's what drove her through the pain. I never knowingly pushed her to do anything she couldn't do, and when I questioned her ability or stamina, she'd just smile sweetly at me and say, "I'm fine, honey, really I am." Occasionally, I would catch her grimace and know that it was time to quit, but even then, she'd often insist on carrying on. She proved to me time and time again, that she was the bravest person I've ever known.

Around Thanksgiving of 1999, we received a call from The Maids franchise headquarters, asking if we would be willing to drive our motor home to San Diego to consult for a start-up The Maids franchise in January of 2000. It took us milliseconds to say, "Yes!" San Diego in the winter? *Hell yes!* We spent Christmas with Mary's family, and left the farm a day or so afterward, our goal being to meet Ken and Linda in Lake Havasu, Arizona, and ring in the millennium together. Unfortunately, Ken's mom took ill and they were unable to make it, but Mary and I followed through with our plan and brought in the year 2000 at the London Bridge. Robert P. McCulloch of chainsaw fame, bought the bridge from London in 1968 and had it disassembled. Each piece was numbered and shipped to Lake Havasu to be reassembled. It spans a canal and links an island with Lake Havasu City, a planned community he began in 1964. The bridge was completed in 1971. It is pared down from its original size, but it is still impressive.

On our way to San Diego, it was decided that we would stop and check out Palm Springs, California, as a potential place to spend the winter as "snowbirds." We were in a camping club at the time, and were unable to get an RV spot in Palm Springs, so we were forced to book in Desert Hot Springs, just outside of town. Desert Hot Springs is not quite as picturesque as Palm Springs, so we took a ride to see the area. I had been to Palm Springs many times before because my employer owned a hotel in Indian Wells, and I had been there for sales meetings. Mary, despite her world travels, had never been to Palm Springs.

Our exploration took us past Outdoor Resort in Cathedral City. We were stunned by the beauty of the parts of this gated resort that we could see from the street. We agreed to come back the next day and see if we could tour the property.

We did just that and met two delightful people who became friends of ours. Phyllis and Bob were two Realtors who sold lots in this five-star RV resort. It was between Palm Springs and Rancho Mirage, the latter being known as the "Playground of Presidents". Palm Springs is the old Hollywood celebrity retreat, but Rancho Mirage has been home to many former presidents, and some very wealthy entrepreneurs, such as Walter and Leonore Annenberg.

Phyllis was just delightful, and we were pleased to learn that she actually appeared in *Gone With The Wind* as the two-year-old Bonnie Blue Butler, sitting on the horse with Clark Gable. Up until her passing a couple of years ago, she was one of only a handful of stars from that movie who was still alive (Olivia de Havilland was one of the others). Phyllis and Mary developed a close relationship, and became very good friends.

Bob gave us the tour of the resort, and showed us the twenty-seven-hole golf course, fourteen tennis courts, eight swimming pools, ten Jacuzzis, and two large clubhouses. We were blown away by the beauty of the place and decided to rent a lot for a month after returning from San Diego. We rented a lot that was for sale, and it turned up sold when we got there, but we stayed on it anyway.

Two days into it, I was convinced that this was where we would spend our winters, and then travel in the summer. I went to aerobics class and jumped around to warm up with the elderly ladies in spandex, then went to the gym and worked out for a couple hours. Mary felt that she wanted to see Florida first, but I convinced her that there was nothing quite like this there, and the weather was far better for her health. After playing some tennis and getting involved in other activities, she was sold on it, so we bought a lot and closed on Valentine's Day in 2000.

I have to admit that during our time there, we had a lot of friends and it was a never ending series of cocktail parties, movie nights, dances, and other social activities. After Mary died, with a few exceptions, all of those invitations dried up. I was no longer part of "John and Mary," so it was as if I no longer existed. I would occasionally see those friends, and there was always a hug and a "How are you doing?", but the invitations stopped coming. I've heard stories of that happening to widows because the remaining wives didn't want a "merry widow" around their husbands, but I think I suffered the same fate, only in reverse. It is a phenomenon that I cannot explain. All I know is that I'm the same person I was when Mary was alive, so I don't know what's changed. Consequently, I had to create a social life beyond the walls of Outdoor Resort, and I did just that.

Outdoor Resort was my home until October of 2012, when I decided that I wanted a house again, and a place that I would not associate with Mary. I needed to concentrate on me, and although I loved Outdoor Resort, I wanted a whole new start.

26

The White House

MARY MEETS PRESIDENT BUSH

It was the summer of 2003, and we were in Chicago to see my family and do some follow-ups with Drs. Rose and Peggy. We were also continuing to treat Mary's painful back problem. Two of her thoracic vertebrae were collapsing; most likely from the massive doses of prednisone she'd been taking as part of her lymphoma treatment. Injections of a plastic substance into the vertebra had only a minimal effect, so it was clear that we had to seek a more invasive solution.

While in Chicago, the phone rang for Mary and it was a representative from Humana Healthcare, her insurance provider. Let me begin by saying that Mary went nose to nose with Humana over claims, payments, and coverage, and probably knew more about their policies than some of their employees. Suffice it to say that she made a name for herself at Humana in Louisville, Kentucky.

The person on the other end of the phone said to Mary, "I know this is short notice, but would you and your husband be able to join us at the White House, as the president announces the Medicare Modernization Act on Monday?" I saw Mary's chin drop, and then a huge smile beamed across her face. "Yes, yes, we can!" was her response. Mary was chosen as one of about six Humana customers to be in the audience in the East Room as the president announced the new legislation.

That following Sunday, Humana flew us to Washington, DC, and put us up at the Hilton. On Monday morning their representative picked us up for breakfast at a restaurant near the White House. We met the other Humana customers, and a few Humana executives, ate breakfast, and then those of us who were capable, walked to the White House. We entered through security at a side entrance, and walked down a long hallway with photos of White House pets of the past, then up a flight of stairs that brought us into the main foyer. The foyer was filled with music being played on a vintage grand piano by a young, uniformed Marine in his dress blues.

We were escorted to the State Dining Room where they were serving a light buffet of finger sandwiches, cookies, and soft drinks. Tuxedoed waiters with white gloves delivered iced tea and lemonade to us and the Beltway elite. There were various members of Congress as well as the other guests of several other health care providers. We were allowed to wander through the various rooms on the first floor of the White House, including the Red and Green rooms, with no velvet ropes to hinder our movements. Young, uniformed service men and women from all the branches of service were present, and I'm sure were keeping a watchful eye on all the guests.

It was announced that the doors to the East Room would open at 2:00 p.m., and the President would arrive at 2:15p.m. A crowd gathered at the doors to the East Room shortly before two, and then the doors were opened. Mary made a beeline for two seats on the center aisle, about three rows back from the podium. The front two rows were reserved for congressmen, the surgeon general, and other dignitaries. Mary sat on the aisle, and I sat next to her. At exactly 2:15p.m., the young service people who lined the main hallway of the White House snapped to attention, and George W. Bush, along with Tommy Thompson walked into the East Room and up to the podium.

The president was introduced by Tommy Thompson and approached the podium. News media cameras were clicking away, and film crews behind us were broadcasting the event for C-Span and the networks. President Bush spoke for approximately thirty minutes, with no teleprompters, introducing special guests and extolling the virtues of the Medicare Modernization

Bill that would provide prescription drug coverage for Medicare patients. For all the criticisms heaped upon George W. Bush, questioning his intelligence, deriding him for his good ol' boy Texas demeanor, and every other derogatory statement made, there stood a man who knew what he was talking about, and did so extemporaneously without the help of electronics. We were thoroughly impressed with our Commander in Chief, and quite proud.

After the president finished speaking, he came off the podium and shook hands with the senators and congressmen in the front rows, then proceeded down the aisle, shaking hands and greeting people along the way. I was standing at the end of our aisle next to Mary, when the president turned to me, shook my hand and said, "How ya' doin'?" in his Texas drawl. I pumped his hand vigorously and said, "Mr. President, we're so proud of you...keep up the good work!" He thanked me, and went across the aisle to shake another hand. He then turned back to us and went right for Mary. She just beamed at him, then he put his arm around her and said, "And how are you doin', young lady?" Mary smiled broadly at him, took his free hand and said, "Oh, Mr. President, give us five more years!" He smiled at her, raised his eyebrows and said, "I'm tryin'!" Then he shook a few more hands and walked down the hall and out of sight.

Unbeknownst to us, my sister Jean was in Chicago taping the event off C-Span. Although she could hear me speak to the president, she could not hear Mary's voice. All she saw was George W. Bush respond to Mary and raise his eyebrows. All Jean could think was, *Oh, my God! What did Mary say to the president?*

As the crowd was mingling, we introduced ourselves to then Senate Majority Leader Bill Frist of Tennessee and Senator Max Baucus of Montana. Mr. Baucus asked us if there was anything we were interested in doing while in DC, and Mary responded that she would like to speak to Iowa Senator Charles Grassley. Senator Baucus said, "Let me see what I can do." Later that day, the Humana representative called to tell us that we had a meeting set up in the late morning with Senator Grassley, the head of the powerful Ways and Means Committee. Humana sent a cab for us after breakfast, and we were taken to the Hart Senate Office Building for our meeting with Senator Grassley.

The Senator only had about thirty minutes before he needed to head to a committee meeting, but he was gracious and accommodating to us. He and Mary talked about farming in Iowa, his wife's struggles with cancer, and

Mary's plight. She impressed upon him how we needed to control health care costs, and the rising cost of prescription drugs. We were all in agreement that something needed to be done, and he thanked us for our input. We felt good about having the opportunity to be heard, and it made for a great day. We enjoyed our time in Washington, DC, but we were unaware that we'd be back there in December.

We were back at Outdoor Resort, enjoying winter in the desert, when we received another phone call from Humana. Once again, we were being invited to return to Washington, DC, to be present for the signing of the Medicare Modernization Act of 2003. Despite Mary's increasing back pain, a team of wild horses could not have prevented her from being there.

Having rid ourselves of most of our winter clothing, we had to go on a search for a trench coat for me, and a pair of appropriate shoes for Mary. They had to be a certain color to match the outfit she was going to wear, and her friend Maryellen volunteered a pair of her cream-colored closed-toed pumps. To this day, Maryellen touts those shoes as "the shoes that met the president." I found an appropriate trench coat, and before we knew it, we were on a plane from Palm Springs to Washington, DC, once again.

We were put up in a hotel much closer to the White House, and the following morning met with the Humana folks at the historic Willard Hotel. The hotel was all decked out for Christmas, and it was a beautiful sight to see. After breakfast, we were divided into groups and put on shuttle buses for the ride to Constitution Hall, where the ceremony was to take place. Mary was to appear onstage with the president, so she rode in a separate bus. I rode with the Humana folks and was seated in a box seat in the theater. I sat there looking out over the audience and noticed how they had bleachers set up behind the president's podium, and then a smaller set of them behind a wooden table where the actual bill signing would take place.

I sat there with the Humana people and watched as a curtain to the right of the stage parted, and a black-suited Secret Service agent, complete with microphone in his ear and a sidearm under his jacket came out briefly, then motioned to someone behind the curtain that it was okay to come onstage. Then out came Mary and another Humana customer, a charming rabbi from somewhere on the East Coast. The Secret Service agent ushered them both to two seats directly behind the podium in the very first row. We all chuckled and speculated about what magic Mary weaved to get herself seated practically within arm's reach of the president! As the rest of the onstage audience came out, we immediately knew why. Just about every one of the other bleacher occupants had either a cane or a walker—effectively, weapons. Mary and the rabbi were the only ones who could walk without some sort of assistance, or literally a weapon with which to strike out at George W. Bush if the impulse struck.

The president came on the stage after everyone was seated, and immediately made a beeline for Mary. He gave her a big hug, and then turned and shook hands with the rabbi. Mary recounted that it was almost as if he remembered her from early in the spring. After a brief speech, the president moved to the wooden desk and signed the bill into law. After doing so the audience erupted into applause, and after briefly shaking some hands, the president left the stage. All of the senators and congressmen continued the handshaking, high-fiving, and backslapping. While this was going on, all the geriatrics from the onstage bleachers began filing out the way they came in...but not Mary. She stood there, looking in the opposite direction of the exiting crowd, toward the senators. We all started buzzing about what she was up to, and I imagine the Secret Service was too. She then, nonchalantly, sashayed over to the cluster of lawmakers and started hugging and shaking hands. Chuck Grassley gave her a big bear hug, and it seemed like Bill Frist and Max Baucus remembered her too. Even Arizona Congressman J.D. Hayworth gave Mary a big bear hug and looked as if he was swallowing her up! All I could think of was the back brace she was wearing and how painful that must have been, but she kept smiling through it all.

We all laughed at how Mary may have found herself a new career...as a Washington lobbyist! The girl was on cloud nine and holding her own with the movers and shakers.

27

Two Inches Taller

ANOTHER AMAZING DOCTOR

The high we were feeling from our visits to Washington, was tempered by the debilitating, painful bouts of back pain that Mary had to endure. We sought the advice of a spine surgeon in Rancho Mirage, Dr. Armen Khachatryan. He was yet another Armenian doctor with the same last name as Dr. Rose, only his was spelled differently. Dr. K, as Mary used to call him was a tall, dark, handsome young man around forty years old. Mary instantly took to him because of his charming bedside manner. As I've said, Mary was a history major in college, so she had a powerful thirst for knowledge, and she happened to be fascinated by the story of the Armenians. Among other things, they discussed the movie *Ararat*, which tells the story of the genocide of the Armenians by the Turks. A brutal event that even now Turkey does not recognize.

We had a lot of faith in Dr. K, and when he told us that Mary needed a corpectomy (replacement of two damaged vertebra with a titanium cage), all Mary could say was, "When do we start? I need relief from this terrible pain." After some routine preoperative tests, Mary was scheduled for the complex surgical procedure in early 2004.

During a pre-op visit, the barely five-foot-tall Mary asked Dr. K if she'd be taller after the surgery. He just smiled at her and said, "Follow me." We followed him into the hallway and he stood Mary up to the doorjamb of the exam room. He told her to stand up straight, then proceeded to draw a line above her head. He wrote, "Mary D" and the date, and said, "We'll just see when you are all healed."

Dr. K performed the surgery with a highly skilled thoracic surgeon named, Dr. Winston. Dr. Winston opened up Mary's chest and cleared the way for Dr. K to install the hollow, telescoping titanium spacer that would take the place of the damaged vertebrae. The spacer was put into place, and crushed bone from one of Mary's ribs was packed inside of it. Another miracle of nature is the bone's ability to fuse together and find a blood supply. Once healed, that bone-filled spacer took the place of the missing vertebrae and several discs, and she lived on minus one rib.

The six hour surgery went smoothly, and a preliminary biopsy of the vertebra showed no signs of lymphoma, despite the opinion of every doctor who viewed the CT scans. They were convinced they would find lymphoma in the marrow of those vertebrae. What they did find was tubercular bacteria called MAC, which is an acronym for Mycobacterium avium complex. This required a long-term regimen of specialized antibiotics, and it was never quite determined how these bacteria found its way into Mary's vertebrae, or if it indeed caused the damage. I have no formal medical training, but I am guessing that it was either introduced during one of several needle biopsies, or during an earlier procedure by a spine doctor in Chicago, who pumped a plastic substance into the vertebrae to shore them up.

I shall never forget how Mary, despite the trauma of the surgery, bounced back as she did. We went for a follow-up visit to Dr. K after Mary was up and around. She could not wait to see if she was taller, so as soon as Dr. K entered the exam room, Mary jumped up and said, "Let's see if I'm taller, Dr. K!" He flashed a broad smile and said, "Okay, you know the drill, Mary." and Mary stood outside the door while he made another mark over her head. She was nearly two inches taller, and when she turned around and looked at the marks, she was practically jumping up and down. I think Dr. K enjoyed that hug she gave him as much as she did.

Dr. K was very concerned as he watched Mary fight for her life toward the end. And he was honored when I asked him to speak at the memorial service I held for her here in the desert, upon my return from the funeral in Iowa. He spoke to the crowd of more than three hundred people of how Mary's faith in him made him a better doctor, and how easing her pain gave him such joy. Everyone could tell that this handsome medical professional truly cared about her and was speaking from his heart. When Dr. Khachatryan spoke to us that day, you could have heard a pin drop because he had everyone's rapt attention.

28

Routine Surgery

WHEN DEATH IS IMMINENT

Having a suppressed immune system caused numerous problems for Mary, and one of the most annoying was the frequent sinus infections she was prone to getting. Sinus infections are particularly difficult to treat because the "bugs" take hold inside the sinus cavity, so antibiotics have a tough time getting to them. After numerous visits to our ENT doctor, Quintin VanDerWerf at Eisenhower Medical Center, and a number of attempts to rid Mary of the infection, he told us that sinus surgery was the most effective way of ridding oneself of this annoying problem. He assured us it was routine surgery and Mary should do just fine.

It was mid-April 2005 when we decided that Mary would undergo the day surgery and be done with this nuisance. We checked into the Day Surgery Center at Eisenhower and Mary was prepped for the thirty-minute procedure. We had no reason to believe that she would not do well, especially since she had that major back surgery in 2003. If she could get through that without complications, why would this be any different?

She was in and out of the operating suite before I knew it, and home in a matter of hours. All went very well, according to Dr. V. Two days later, just after we kissed our snowbird neighbors, Dick and Carol, good-bye, Mary began to feel quite ill. She had an uncanny knack for knowing how she felt or how she should feel, and this time she said, "Johnny, I need to get to the ER right away," I knew better than to question her because she had been right so many times before. Mary was never one to cry wolf, and she was anything but a hypochondriac.

I drove her to the ER and got a wheelchair because she was so weak at that point, she could barely get out of the car. She deteriorated right before my eyes, and I tried desperately to hide the fear that was building inside of me.

The intake nurse took Mary's vital signs and immediately had her put in a room. The doctor came in shortly and questioned me as to what may have caused her condition. I briefly explained her medical history and her recent sinus surgery. I also made it a point to tell the ER doctor that Mary had been seeing an infectious disease doctor by the name of Dr. Cone. I did that because I sensed there was an infection running rampant through Mary's bloodstream.

Her vitals continued to deteriorate, and it was clear to me by the amount of attention she was getting, that this was not good. Dr. Cone suddenly appeared to assess Mary's condition and ordered that she be immediately put on a respirator. I'm sure all the blood drained from my brain as I heard his order, and I had to sit down to prevent fainting from the shock. I was asked to leave the room after speaking to Mary before they put in the breathing tube. She was barely conscious, but I told her I loved her and would be there when she woke up. I told her not to worry because she'd been through much worse than this. She smiled at me and whispered, "I love you too, honey." Our dear friend C.J., who had come down to the ER to be with me, spoke softly to Mary and said a little prayer with her. We were then asked to leave the room while they inserted the respiration tube.

She lapsed into a coma shortly thereafter, so those were the last words I was to hear from her for nearly a month. I heard the word *sepsis* just as Dr. VanDerWerf came into the room. He told me that the ER staff brought him up to speed and that he was involved with her care. He apologized profusely and said this wasn't supposed to happen because everything was done by the book and with extra precautions because of Mary's condition.

I didn't blame him, but I couldn't help but wonder why he would recommend surgery for someone like Mary. This one came back to bite him.

I was told that Mary's vitals had deteriorated so dramatically that she was being taken up to the cardiac care unit, and was in septic shock. As they worked on Mary, I went outside to call her sisters and my siblings to let them know what was happening. I was so scared, my hands were shaking and I could hardly dial my cell phone.

My first call was to her sister Phyllis. When I heard her cheerful voice, I just fell apart and could hardly articulate what was happening. She did her best to calm me down, but as I explained the gravity of the situation, the fear she felt grew inside of her. Phyllis pledged to spread the word within the family and immediately started making plans to fly out to Palm Springs. Within days, Phyllis, Jane, and many of the nieces and nephews were at my side.

Mary was stabilized, and then taken up to the cardiac intensive care unit at Eisenhower because her heart was in a precarious state. I was told to wait in the CICU waiting room while they got Mary into a special room within the unit. By that time, our dear friend Margie and her sister Rae showed up to sit with me. There's nothing like seeing a familiar face when you're alone, scared, and dealing with a health crisis.

When I was finally able to see her, I walked into a CICU room and saw my dear, sweet Mary lying there hooked up to no less than nine IVs and any number of electronic monitoring systems. Her vitals were crashing, body systems were shutting down, and the prognosis was poor. One of the most critical vital signs in cases of sepsis is blood pressure. The nurses were having a tough time getting any blood pressure readings, so Dr. Cone had them start her on a new drug called Xigris. It's a drug used only when death is imminent in sepsis patients.

Over the next couple of days, concerned friends and my sisters-in-law all arrived to be with me as Mary clung to life. Even most of my Iowa nieces and nephews flew in because of fear that Aunt Mary may not make it. My nephew Nicholas came down from San Francisco and slept on the floor of the Cardiac Critical Care Unit waiting room just so he could be near his favorite aunt.

I was allowed to sit with Mary for only short periods of time as the Critical Care nurses adjusted IV drips, and managed the nine tubes going into Mary's body. I likened them to orchestra conductors as they constantly made refinements in an effort to keep her blood pressure at a safe level. During sepsis, cells leak fluid through their membranes, causing a fatal loss of blood pressure, also known as septic shock. Low blood pressure keeps oxygen from reaching vital organs, and they begin to shut down. The liver and kidneys are particularly vulnerable. Her blood pressure stopped crashing after the Xigris was started, but her heart was struggling to keep her alive. The cardiologist ordered an echocardiogram to measure the efficiency of her heart, and since my sister-in-law Jane is an echo tech, he invited her in to look at the tapes. He discussed the films with Jane and agreed that Mary's heart was indeed in a bad way, and they would need to adjust the medications to help it along. Jane confided in me months later that it was the worst heart echo she'd ever seen, and she was truly terrified afterward, but she did not let me know.

Once Mary was stabilized, but certainly not out of the woods, she was transferred to the Critical Care Unit because of the sepsis. It was a concern having a possibly contagious patient in a Cardiac Care Unit.

The Eisenhower Medical Center Critical Care Unit staff, led by Lisa Berg, RN, is a remarkable group of professionals who worked around the clock to make sure Mary would survive. A desk was set up outside the door of Mary's private room, and meticulous records and charts were maintained so each shift change would be seamless.

As each day ticked by, a steady stream of friends and neighbors brought food and comfort to my family and me as we rotated our vigil between Mary's room and the Critical Care Waiting Room. There was, at times, more food than we could eat, and so many well-wishers that it was almost overwhelming.

Someone gave me a journal, and it was used daily so friends could write notes of encouragement for Mary and me. In their notes to Mary, they expressed love and affection, support, and offered humorous observations of what was going on as Mary's body struggled to stay alive. As the days wore on, she slowly began to improve, but her kidneys were lagging, so it was decided that she would be hooked up to continuous kidney dialysis. In order to do so, it was necessary to have ports surgically implanted in the arteries of her upper legs. A surgeon was called in to insert the ports at her bedside.

I was at her bedside, along with Phyllis on Mary's birthday, May 5, when she regained consciousness and opened her eyes. It was the first time since I took her to the ER, more than a month ago. Phyllis and I wept with joy as Mary reconnected with us visually, but could not speak because she was still on a respirator. We immediately told the nurses that she was awake, and they arranged to get the doctor's permission to remove the breathing tube. After the tube was removed, she looked me in the eyes, smiled broadly, and squeaked out the words, "Hi. Johnny!" I fell apart. I was overjoyed that she would choose to open her eyes on her birthday! It was a magical and emotional moment for all three of us.

It is fitting that I say a word about my dear sister-in-law, Phyllis Jacobsen. Throughout the worst of times, she was the person I could most rely on. She was there when Mary had the initial facial surgery (after which she was diagnosed with non-Hodgkin's lymphoma), there to hold my hand while Mary was in isolation during the bone marrow transplant, and there countless other times when I needed her strong moral support. She loved Mary dearly, and even when she felt as helpless as I did, knowing that there was only so much we could do for her, she turned to me and knew what I needed most—whether it was a sandwich because I hadn't eaten, or a shoulder to cry on.

I am in awe of Phyllis's capacity for love and caring. She spent count-less hours away from her kids and husband Dennis, primarily because her bonds of family were so strong, and her sister needed her. When there was some thought that a sister might make a bone marrow donor, Phyllis never hesitated to get tested. Unfortunately, none of Mary's sisters were a match.

Joe and Amelia Kasper hit a home run when they gave birth to Phyllis. The same wholesome Iowa upbringing, that made Mary who she was, shaped Phyllis as well. I have always felt close to Phyllis, but after Mary's ordeal, and witnessing Phyllis's undying devotion to her sister, and her love for me, I feel truly blessed to be a part of her family. I adore her children, my niece and nephews, as they do me. When I come back to the farm in West Branch, I am truly coming home.

29

Proceed With Caution

THE ROAD AHEAD

Mary bounced back quickly from her near-death experience, and while she lay in her hospital room recovering, we decided that it was time to stop traveling and remain close to the doctors in Palm Springs. The prospect of staying home all day during the summer was not appealing to me, plus the cost of my own health insurance was becoming a burden on our finances, which were already strained by some of the costs we incurred for Mary outside of Medicare.

I opened up the newspaper as I sat there keeping Mary company, and decided to peruse the want ads. Lo and behold, the Westin Mission Hills was looking for a concierge in Rancho Mirage. Given my years of sales and marketing experience in the travel industry, this seemed like a good fit for me. I applied and was called in for an interview. I was immediately hired and started working in the summer of 2005. Mary was feeling so well, she decided that she would go back to Iowa to visit her sisters and see her old friends. I kissed her good-bye and stayed behind to work and take care of the dog. Her trip back home turned into a five-week hiatus, which included a trip up to Minneapolis with her old gal pals, and a visit to my sisters and nieces in Chicago. After seeing Mary near death just weeks before, and knowing that her health was so fragile, I began to worry that this time away from me might be precious time we'd lose forever.

When Mary returned to me, I told her that she was never going to be away from me that long again. I told her it gave me a taste of what life would be like without her, and I did not like it one bit! It may sound self-ish on my part, but perhaps I had an ominous premonition that I did not want to face.

That following spring, nearly a year after her near fatal bout of sepsis, Mary went in for routine blood work. She was feeling fine, but it was something lymphoma patients have come to expect as they live with their disease. The call from the doctor's office came a day or so later; it was an urgent message from Mary's oncologist, telling her to come in as soon as possible. There was an anomaly in her test results they needed to discuss with us.

We called and made an appointment for that next day, which they had no problem confirming. That was the first red flag. We were put in an exam room and waited for Dr. Vafai to come in. I turned to Mary and told her that whatever this was, we're in this together and we'd be fine. Just a few minutes later, he walked in the door, and although he didn't have the best bedside manner, he looked genuinely concerned as he greeted us. Mary was the first to say, "What's wrong, Dr. Vafai? I have a bad feeling about this." There was noticeable concern in her voice. He responded, "Mary, your white cell count is elevated, how do you feel?" She responded that she felt a bit fatigued, but otherwise fine.

That response probably confirmed what the doctor expected, and he shared his concern with us right then and there. He said that in a healthy person, an elevated white count can simply mean there is an active infection and the body is trying to combat it by creating more disease-fighting white cells. If that were indeed the case, Mary would have been running a fever and she would have felt ill. This result was much more ominous. We asked the doctor not to sugarcoat his suspicions, so he complied and told us flat out, "You most likely have a pre-leukemic condition called MDS, myelo-dysplastic syndrome." He went on to explain that this is a common side effect of a bone marrow transplant and chemotherapy over the years. When this is discovered in patients with Mary's history, the prognosis is poor. That news hit us like a ton of bricks, and as I struggled to catch my breath and respond, Mary chimed in and said, "Okay, Doc. What do we need to do?" She had a huge smile on her face. For a brief moment, I thought to myself, *"How can she be so matter of fact about this?"*. Now I know: she was my Mary, the girl who had endured so much bad news over the years, and lived to tell about it. She was sure she would beat this one too.

The doctor told her there would be more blood work and yet another bone marrow biopsy to confirm his suspicions, and then he would put her on a regimen of a chemotherapy drug called Vidaza, which is used to fight MDS. He again underscored the fact that post-bone marrow transplant patients, who are diagnosed with MDS, do not routinely have a good outcome.

We left the doctor's office with another heavy burden on our shoulders, but if my memory serves me, we went out for dinner and reaffirmed our will to fight yet again.

Mary went through more tests and endured yet another bone marrow biopsy so we could move forward with treatment. It broke my heart each time she was forced to suffer through this necessary, but barbaric procedure. She would have to lie on her side with her bare hip exposed, while the doctor proceeded to bore into her iliac crest (the crown of the pelvis) to remove core samples of the marrow within. Despite copious amounts of local anesthesia, the pressure and clear discomfort is difficult to watch. But I was always there holding her hand and talking to her throughout the procedure. Some doctors made me wear a mask and gloves, but I didn't care. My concern was with that sweet, wonderful girl who did not deserve to suffer in this way.

The bone marrow biopsy confirmed the doctor's worst fears. Mary had advanced MDS, and without intervention, it would result in full-blown ALL, or acute lymphocytic leukemia. That is another life-threatening disease, which is difficult to treat, let alone cure. The only real chance of a cure was another bone marrow transplant. Mary started on the Vidaza and went weekly to the doctor's infusion center for her treatments.

In the meantime, I did some research on the City of Hope in Los Angeles and found out that they were a world-renowned leader in bone marrow transplantation. We quickly made an appointment for an evaluation. We fired up our motor home and drove to a nearby Elks Club to overnight in advance of our appointment. The folks at the Elks were so supportive and caring when they found out our reason for being there, some even offering to drive us there and back. We were overwhelmed by their concern and to this day I cannot think of City of Hope without remembering their kindness.

We met with a female oncologist who was sympathetic to our plight, and upon examining Mary, remarked that she expected to see a "sick" person, not someone as perky and bright, as Mary was that day. She even remarked on how colorful her outfit was—not the drab look of a sick person who was possibly facing her end of days.

The doctor ran a series of blood tests and requested Mary's medical records to help them reach a decision. Unfortunately, a few days later we received a call from the doctor saying that Mary's prognosis was so poor, and considering her age and prior treatment history, she was a very poor candidate for another bone marrow transplant. A friend once asked her if she could endure another transplant, her response was, "If it would allow me even a few more years with my Johnny…yes, I would do it in a heartbeat!" All she ever wanted was to be at my side, and that's where I wanted her to stay.

We returned to our place with heavy hearts, not knowing what the months ahead would bring. Mary went in dutifully for her chemotherapy, and initially showed some improvement, but the doctor knew that her prognosis remained poor, at best.

On May 17, 2006, we celebrated our twentieth wedding anniversary by having a candlelight dinner at a fine dining restaurant in Palm Desert, called Jillian's. It was a romantic dinner with good food and good wine, and I know that Mary thoroughly enjoyed it. I did because she was sitting across the table from me. At one point during dinner, she leaned over to me and whispered, "I'm going to be here to celebrate our twenty-fifth anniversary, honey!" She smiled sweetly at me and I simply replied, "Yes, dear, you will. I know you will." I was crying inside because I knew the road ahead was bleak.

Weeks went by and people in our resort started leaving for the summer. The snowbirds left as soon as the thermometer flirted with triple-digit temperatures. Our neighbors, and dear friends Dick and Carol, were no exceptions. They were off on another summer adventure to the East Coast, and were anxious to get moving. The day they left, Mary was not feeling well, but she put on her bathrobe and went outside to kiss them good-bye. Little did they know that, that was the last time they would see Mary.

After they drove off in their motor home, Mary turned to me and said, "Johnny, I need to go to the hospital." I knew she wasn't well, and I'd learned over the years that when Mary said she wasn't feeling well, she was sick. We called the doctor's office and he told us to take Mary to Eisenhower Medical Center. We had her there within a couple of hours, and once she was comfortable in her room, they started hooking up IVs and taking blood. Her white cell count was off the charts. Our worst fears were confirmed, Mary was suffering from acute lymphocytic leukemia, and we needed to intervene right away. She was immediately placed on IV antibiotics, hydration, and it was decided that she needed to have bedside apheresis to remove the excess white cells her body was producing. The cells being produced in such numbers were defective and unable to perform their disease-fighting duty. They were simply crowding out her red cells and platelets.

As always, I was with Mary as often as I could be while keeping my job. On one such occasion, I was sitting there with Mary when a nurse came in to give her scheduled medication. I had not seen her before, so I watched as she readied the various pills and injectable drugs she was preparing. One of the drugs prescribed was heparin; an anticoagulant used to "Hep Lock" her infusion port after flushing it with saline. I personally performed this very task many times at home, so I was keenly aware of its purpose.

Mary was hooked up to the apheresis machine through her port, so I knew it wasn't time for the heparin, but I watched as the nurse prepared the syringe. I asked her why she was readying the heparin, and she proceeded to tell me that Mary was supposed to get it every four hours. I responded, "No, she's only supposed to get heparin to lock her port after flushing it." I reminded her that Mary's red cell and platelet counts were dangerously low and introducing heparin into her IV line was dangerous. She ignored me and proceeded to stick the syringe into the cannula of Mary's IV line. Once again, I told her not to give Mary any heparin until I could verify it with her doctor. She once again ignored my plea, and while looking me straight in the eye, she pushed down on the plunger and delivered the dose directly into Mary's port, and directly into her heart.

I screamed at her to get out of the room, so she ran out into the hall wide-eyed at my outburst. I got on the phone and demanded to speak to the director of the nursing staff. A woman came on and I very forcefully told her what happened and who the nurse was. She told me that that particular nurse was having personal problems, and that she would look into it. She assured me that the heparin would not harm Mary (I'm still not convinced of that), but I insisted that the nurse be taken off Mary's case, and later found out that the nurse was suspended. I was vindicated, and I was right. I'm not even in the medical profession and I knew I was right. I was Mary's advocate that day, as I had always been.

30

Hospice

COME FLY WITH ME

Mary's condition deteriorated despite the best efforts of her doctor and the nursing staff.

One of the side effects of the massive doses of antibiotics Mary was getting in her IV was hearing loss. The poor girl was having a difficult time hearing, especially when there was ambient noise in the room. She underwent daily, bedside apheresis to keep her white count down, and allow her red cells to do their job without being crowded out.

I was relieved when Phyllis and Jane flew out in the heat of late June and early July to be with me and help out. Their presence allowed me to go back to work for a few days, just so I could get away from the situation and keep some sense of normalcy in my life. I didn't like being away from Mary, because I felt like I was giving up precious minutes with her, but being with my good friends at work helped me a great deal. Three of them, Sheri, Karen, and Shan, came to know Mary and grew to love her. Mary would come to the hotel and sit in the lobby reading the newspaper when I had to work a late shift, just to be near me and keep me company. My coworkers thought that was very sweet, so it endeared her to them.

I went back to my job at the Westin as a concierge and Marketing Coordinator for their timeshare program. My job was to perform concierge services and sign qualified people up to do the timeshare presentation, in hopes that they will buy. There I was, just back from work after leaving my dying wife, just trying to get some normalcy back into my life to help me deal with the stress, only to be knocked back down by a shallow, nihilistic woman who stood before me. I was working the early shift so that I could be at the hospital in the afternoon. As I sat at my desk around 8:30 a.m., a woman, obviously frazzled over something, stood in front of me, red-faced and loaded for bear. In my usually cheerful manner, I offered my assistance. She leaned over the desk and screamed into my face, "How the hell do I get a fucking newspaper in this place?" The Westin is very focused on the guest experience, so with aplomb I responded to her rudeness by saying, "I'm very sorry that your newspaper wasn't at your doorstep this morning, let me see if I can locate one for you." I had to walk away from the bitch just to preserve my sanity and avoid saying something I would regret. I went into the lobby bar and looked for the stack of morning newspapers that were usually sitting on the sideboard, but there were none. I then walked over to the bellman's stand at the porte cochere, but they were also out of them. It was as though the Universe was conspiring to keep this woman in my face! I returned to my desk to find her there, red-faced, arms crossed, and practically tapping her feet. When I arrived empty-handed, I could see her blood pressure rising.

I very calmly told the insolent shrew that there was a large group in house, and perhaps the group leaders may have taken additional copies of the newspaper to breakfast (which was a plausible, but "off the top of my head" fabrication), and then offered to have one immediately sent to her room. She glared at me and said, "That's what I thought you'd say to me! Don't bother; you're useless!" then stormed out of the lobby. I sat down in my chair and could feel the emotion build up inside me, and I fought back tears. I struggled to compose myself, but Carol at the front desk knew what I was going through, and could see the pain in my face. I thought to myself, *Here I am, struggling with the impending death of the most important person in my life, and I have to bite my tongue and be polite to a spoiled "princess" brat who made a mountain out of a molehill over a fucking morning copy of* USA Today! Carol's hug helped calm me down.

The next day, I was sitting in the hospital lobby, eating a sandwich the girls from work brought me, when the doctor walked up to me with a very somber look on his face. The girls excused themselves, as Dr. Vafai sat down with Phyllis and me. He delivered the news that I knew was coming, but dreaded to hear. Mary's most recent blood tests came back, and clearly showed that the leukemia was raging out of control, despite the medical team's best efforts.

The doctor said that we could go at it with aggressive chemotherapy, but it would only delay the inevitable, and make her last days miserable. My heart sank when he recommended hospice for Mary. Phyllis and I both broke down in tears at this news, and the doctor asked if I would like to be the one to tell Mary. I said that I would because that kind of news should only be delivered by a loved one.

Jane was sitting with Mary, so Phyllis asked Jane to step out into the hall and I went back into the room and sat down on a chair next to Mary's bed. I grasped her hand and told her I had something very important to discuss with her. She smiled sweetly as I explained to her that the test results were not good, and that her condition had deteriorated dramatically.

At that point, despite my best efforts to be brave, I became quite emotional and struggled with telling her that the doctor recommended hospice care for her. After eighteen years of offering her hope for the future, I was the one telling her that the end was near, and it was one of the most difficult things I've ever had to do. Her lower lip quivered, but she continued to smile at me while I choked back tears. She said, "It's okay, honey. I'm tired; I can't do this anymore…it's over, but that's okay." As she spoke, she was stroking my head, consoling me, and bravely facing the harsh reality of it all.

She spoke about her eighteen-year battle, and confided in me that she knew she was facing the end, ever since the doctor called us that day in March to tell us that she had MDS. In retrospect, she was incredibly brave that day after basically being told to get your affairs in order because you're going to die. At that point she became almost serene, as if a great weight had been lifted from her shoulders. She knew that there would be no more harsh chemotherapy, no more painful bone marrow biopsies, no more fights with insurance companies, and no more worrying *me*. Her only concern was leaving me…alone.

Her greatest fear was that I would be alone once she was gone, so she made me promise her that I would be happy—whatever that meant. I made that promise to her.

The following day we talked about hospice, and the doctor arranged for a man to come by and talk to us about the hospice services available in the area. Well, this salesman (that's what he was), from a local hospice center in Rancho Mirage showed up at about 11p.m., to tell us about the hospice care they provide outside the home. He stood over Mary's bed touting his wonderful "hotel-like" hospice center and all the wonderful services they provide to the dying. Mary was getting visibly annoyed because he was not directing anything to her, and because she was having difficulty hearing, she missed much of what he was saying. She finally got her dander up enough to shout, "Look, buddy, I'm the one who's dying here! Talk to me!"

He got the message, and started addressing her. Even days before she died, she had the fire within to get her point across!

Earlier that day we talked about where Mary would like to be when the end came. She understood that you couldn't set up hospice in a motor home, so she was resigned to the fact that she'd have to go somewhere. I was not. I wanted her to be on her sister Phyllis's farm in West Branch, a place she considered home.

I told that to the hospice center salesman in the hallway, and he suggested that I bring Mary to his place; they'd get her stabilized, and then arrange for an air ambulance to take her to the farm. I said no, and told him that she was stable now, and without that supportive care, I didn't know how long she might have. I could not take the chance and let her die in a strange place. I thanked him for coming, but declined his offer.

I went home that night and got on the Internet to find an air ambulance company. I found one and paid $15,000 to charter a Learjet to fly Mary to the farm. I also ordered a beautiful, handmade walnut box for her ashes, made by the New Melleray Abbey monks in Iowa, who are known for their fine urns and caskets. On that Wednesday, I came to the hospital with a picture of the urn and to tell Mary that she was going home to Iowa. I told her that I had chartered an air ambulance, and we would leave on Friday morning, July 7, 2006. I also told her that I ordered the walnut urn, and the good news was that it was built for two…so we would spend eternity in a "double-wide." She laughed at the not-so-loosely veiled reference to our RV lifestyle.

Mary was so excited to be going home, she'd tell everyone who came into the room, "I'm going home to Iowa on Friday!" Just the thought made her deliriously happy, and took all the pain and fear off of her face.

On that Friday morning, the ambulance arrived to take us to the Palm Springs Airport.

The charge nurse on the third floor was Lynne, and she seemed to bond with Mary, attending to her every need. She, and the entire staff at EMC were so good to Mary; I'll never forget their kindness.

———

Even now, seven years after Mary's passing, people at EMC remember Mary. I recently had to have surgery for a kidney stone that was stuck in my ureter, and when they wheeled me into pre-op and parked me in a cubicle, I looked across the room at the nurse's station and saw a blonde nurse. With a heavy Kiwi accent, she pointed her finger at me and said, "You're Mary's husband!" I was incredulous, and you could have knocked me over with a feather. Her name was Karen, and she remembered Mary after nearly seven years. She told me that she often thought of Mary, and remembered her as a very strong woman. Any apprehension or fear I had, melted away, and the young nurse who was putting in my IV line said to me, "Wow, your wife must have been someone really special." I replied, "Yes, she was." I could feel a tear running down my cheek.

On the day I was to be released, my nurse was none other than Lynne. She walked into my room and immediately came over and gave me a big, warm hug. I asked if she remembered Mary and me, and she said, "God, yes! Mary was in room 380." She was exactly right. She was amazed that it had been nearly seven years, but she said she remembers her as if it were yesterday. Despite not remembering the destination, she did remember that I flew Mary back home via air ambulance.

It never ceases to amaze me how Mary touched so many lives in her fifty-eight years on this planet.

———

We arrived at the General Aviation Terminal and drove right up to the waiting Learjet. On board was a flight nurse, and a respiratory therapist, all shoehorned into the tiny jet. Our close friend Bob was there with camera at the ready to chronicle our departure. I still don't know how he got himself onto the tarmac, but I was glad to see him. Another friend, Linda, stood waving at the fence and watched as her dear friend Mary was put onboard. Linda told me later that she could barely see through her tears of both sadness and joy. She was so happy to see Mary going home, but she knew she'd never see her again.

We got Mary comfortable onto the gurney inside the Lear, and I sat in the very tail of the plane so I could see her face as she lay facing me. She was fully aware that she was about to take the last flight of her life, and that it was a fitting end for someone who spent her adult life in the travel industry, and had flown around the world on her own.

The Learjet taxied to the runway and streaked off into the clear Palm Springs sky, on its way to Cedar Rapids, Iowa. At over 500 miles per hour, the 2,100-mile trip took only a little more than three hours. It was a bit noisy, but comfortable. Mary drifted in and out of sleep, and would occasionally turn to the flight nurse and ask, "Where's my dog?" We had discussed the possibility of taking our cocker spaniel, Austin, with us on the plane, but it was much too small to accommodate his kennel.

We rescued the sweet little black cocker from the Cathedral City dog pound a year prior. After getting a blood draw at a Rancho Mirage lab, we decided to go to the Japanese restaurant for lunch. We sat in the window eating our Bento lunch, and saw the nurse that had just drawn Mary's blood come into the parking lot with a beautiful black cocker on a leash. The supermarket cart boy was petting him and giving him a treat, and I remarked, "Isn't he an adorable cocker?". Mary agreed and said we should consider another dog after having put Lady down about two years prior. We thought nothing more about it until after lunch when we went to the market to pick up a few groceries. As we entered, I saw the cart boy and said, "Hey, that was a cute cocker you were petting", and he replied, "Yeah, it's so sad. She's taking him to the pound because she can't find a home for him". We were crushed. I immediately tried to call the blood lab, but they were closed for lunch, and she was at the pound already. We raced down there and saw Austin, freshly groomed and wearing a kerchief, shivering with sorrowful eyes in a cage amidst howling pitbulls and strays. It broke our hearts, but after some fancy talking and a phone call to the nurse, we were able to adopt him. That little guy bonded with Mary and consoled her through her final year on this earth.

On that fateful day, we left Austin in the able care of our friends Gary and Ken, who were happy to do that for us.

When we arrived in Cedar Rapids, an ambulance was waiting for us on the tarmac. The ride from the airport to the farm was only about forty-five minutes, so we were there by around 4p.m. Mary's sisters were flying back commercially, so they would not arrive until later that evening, after Mary had fallen asleep. They had pretty much said good-bye at the hospital before we flew back in the air ambulance.

The ambulance backed down the driveway, and when they opened the back doors, Mary could see the farmhouse, the dogs, and some of our nieces and nephews waiting there for her. She had the biggest grin on her face when she saw all the things she loved. That image is forever etched in my brain.

Iowa City Hospice had delivered the hospital bed and supplies to the farm, however, a special mattress pad had not yet arrived. We made Mary comfortable by sitting her up in the regular double bed in that same large bedroom.

My nephew John's wife, Christine, was in medical school at the time, so she took control of the situation and made sure Mary's medical needs were met, that all the medications and supplies were there, and that Mary got something to eat. I breathed a sigh of relief knowing that she was so well cared for by the people she loved. She was hungry, so we gave her some chicken soup and crackers, and my brother-in-law's sister, Kathleen, spoon-fed her as Mary laughed and joked with the kids.

Our nephew John Dennis appeared at the door of the bedroom, so Kathleen said, "Mary, look who's here!" She looked up to see her favorite nephew (whoever was present was her favorite at that time), smiled a big smile, and said, "Like I care?" He came over and gave her a big kiss and hug. She was a queen holding court that day; delighted to be there. Mary was never happier than she was when those kids were around, so having them around during her final hours was very comforting for her. She knew her time on this earth was limited, but I think she'd come to terms with that, and decided that she would let nature takes its course.

The foam mattress arrived, and after the bed was put back together, I said to Mary, "Honey, you're getting pretty droopy. It's been a long day. Why don't we get you in bed now?" I then asked if she'd like me to carry her to the bed, but she insisted on going on her own steam. We stood her up and she was a bit shaky, but she held on to me by grabbing onto my forearms. I remember how she flashed me the biggest smile because despite being so weak, she was able to stand. She always celebrated minor victories—that's the kind of person she was. I slowly started backing up and she followed along, shuffling her feet. We were only going about six feet, but she still had to stop midway to regain her strength. Clearly, the leukemia was raging, and her vital red cells were unable to deliver enough oxygen to her blood because they were being crowded out by her rampaging white cells. That was also clearly evident because as she stood up, and blood was rushing to her extremities, she began to get disoriented, and started speaking gibberish. I got her to the bed, and sat her down, then she looked up at me and said, "I need a table." We brought one over and she just stared at it. She was terribly confused at that point.

It was about 8 p.m. We got her situated in the bed and covered her up so she could take a much-needed nap. I stroked her forehead, and said, "I love you, honey...you need to take a nap now." She replied, "I love you, Johnny." Those were the last words I would hear her speak.

She quickly fell asleep, and then lapsed into a coma. By midnight, her breathing became labored as her lungs filled with fluid. I panicked, thinking we hadn't given her the proper pain management meds, so I called the hospice nurse. She said she was about an hour away, but she'd get there as soon as possible. Approximately an hour later, she made it to the farm, and I felt terrible dragging her out of her house at midnight. She had to be about seven months pregnant, and clearly uncomfortable, but she took one look at Mary and said, "I'm sorry, Mr. DiViggiano, Mary is in her final hours. That sound she makes when she breathes is called the death rattle. Her lungs are filling with fluid." She wasn't telling me anything I didn't already know. As her chemotherapy-damaged heart was failing to move blood through her system, fluid was building up in her lungs, and she was, for all intents and purposes, drowning. It may sound like a gruesome statement, but it is the physiology of the dying process. Her kidneys were probably shutting down as well, further exacerbating the situation. The nurse put more morphine drops under her tongue to help ease her breathing, and I crawled into her hospital bed and cradled her in my arms.

I stroked her hair and spoke to her all night long. I had a one-sided conversation with my true love, and retold stories that she shared with me over the years, many of which I've put down on these pages. I reminded her of how much I loved her, and how her love for me made me a better person. I spoke of how I would love her until the day I died, and that I hoped we'd see each other in another place. I've always heard that a person in a coma can hear what you're saying, so I poured my heart out to her. My mouth was next to her left ear, so I whispered those loving words, hoping she would take them with her to the other side.

I wasn't alone in the bedroom during her final minutes. Her sisters Phyllis and Jane came in after I called to them when the time between her breaths lengthened. Mary took her last breath and died in my arms at 5:25 a.m., on July 8, 2006. The twenty-six wonderful years of my life with Mary ended at that moment.

To say that I was overcome with emotion would be a gross understatement; my life as I knew it was over. A shroud of grief descended over me like a cloak, and I began to cry. As I choked back my tears I said, "It's okay, honey. It's okay to go. You fought long and hard and you deserve to rest. I love you, sweetheart, and I always will."

The girls were in tears, and said their good-byes to their big sister, but soon their attention turned to me. They came around the bed to my side and gently moved my arm out from under Mary's head, gently set her back down, and then encouraged me to get up. My right arm was so numb, it just hung limply as I tried to get up. I tried to stand, but I was so stiff I couldn't straighten up right away. I was stuck in that semi-fetal position for about six hours. I had a full bladder, but I did not want to leave Mary's side. I felt like the faithful dog that will not leave the side of his beloved companion, but nature wasn't about to let me ignore my need to void.

Mary's bone marrow transplant doctor, Dr. Rose Catchatourian, was in Iowa City that weekend visiting her daughter who was a student at the University of Iowa, Mary's alma mater. I had been in contact with her, and I told her that I was flying Mary back to the farm, so she asked if she could come and see her on Saturday. Early Saturday morning, I called Dr. Rose and told her that Mary had passed. After offering her sincere condolences, she said, "John, I'd like to come by the farm anyway, and see you." I was touched that Rose would want to do that for me, and I welcomed her to come by. She arrived just minutes after the funeral director left the house with Mary's remains.

I have the utmost respect for Rose as a doctor, and I love her as a human being. I immediately broke down as I greeted her at the door. This diminutive woman, who is a giant in the world of bone marrow transplantation, gave me a big bear hug and led me to the sofa. She said something to me that cut through my grief and consoled me on the spot. She said, "John, there is nothing more you could have done for Mary. You did everything humanely possible, and your efforts extended her life by many, many years." Hearing that from a medical professional of her stature, carved away the guilt and worries about whether or not I did all that I could. From her perspective, and after treating thousands of patients, it was her considered opinion that I did a yeoman's job in caring for Mary. Like none she'd ever seen before. Her statement lightened a heavy heart, at least for the moment.

I am friends with Rose to this day, and whenever I'm in Chicago, and her busy schedule allows, I will meet with Rose, Dr. Peggy Telfer, and sometimes Rose's husband, Dr. Paul Ruestow for dinner. I enjoy the company of these wonderful medical professionals, who always thought I should go to medical school. I seemed to have impressed them with my thirst for knowledge about Mary's non-Hodgkin's lymphoma and my undying efforts to keep her alive.

31

Good-bye, My Love

AN IOWA FAREWELL

The preparations for Mary's funeral went into high gear. I knew that I wanted our dear friend C.J. Wright to come to Iowa to perform the spiritual portion of Mary's funeral. She is a Unity Village minister, a close friend of ours, and a former resident of Hawaii. I wanted a Hawaiian-themed service, since my career with Hawaii travel was such a big part of our lives together. I called C.J. and she was honored to be asked, so I arranged to fly her to Iowa from her home in Oregon.

Our good friends in Iowa City, Julie and Kevin Monson, offered the use of their family's restored nineteenth-century barn for the funeral luncheon. They restored this magnificent structure and use it for family functions, but were happy to offer it for Mary, because they knew how much she loved the stately structure. Since the funeral was to be in July, and in anticipation of warm weather, someone came up with the idea of making fans with Mary's photograph on them. Julie immediately offered to get them made, and called in some favors with her printer.

Phyllis and I met with Julie and Kevin at their place to look at the barn and decided how we'd set up the funeral luncheon, which was catered by the local Hy-Vee grocery store. There was a side portion of the barn where Kevin parked his John Deere tractor, and he said that he'll move the tractor and hide it somewhere, so we could set up the buffet tables in there. To that, I immediately said, "No, Kevin, please don't hide the tractor. I'd like you to park it right out front of the barn so everyone can see it! Mary loved tractors and yours looks like it just came out of the showroom!" Kevin is a highly regarded architect in Iowa City by trade, and also a gentleman farmer who happened to take great pride in his tractor. It had to be the cleanest and most pampered tractor in all of Iowa. Kevin agreed to have the tractor cleaned and polished, and placed right outside the deck that faced east toward the cornfields of Iowa. As the old saying says, "Corn is knee-high by the Fourth of July," and 2006 was no exception. The corn was deep green and lush in the distance, which made for a bucolic and peaceful backdrop for the funeral service to come.

Mary's wish was to be cremated and buried on her sister's farm in West Branch, so we chose a spot in the grove of trees to the west of the house, overlooking a magnificent expanse of Iowa farmland.

The funeral services were arranged with family friend and funeral director Michael Lensing of Iowa City. Michael personally planned funeral services for my in-laws, Amelia and Joe Kasper, and has known the Kasper family for many, many years. He and my sister-in-law Jane had been close friends as well. Michael met with Phyllis, Jane, and I and we arranged all the details to make Mary's funeral service memorable. For the viewing I rented a beautiful mahogany casket, and chose one of Mary's handmade pink dresses for her to wear. It was agreed that a one-night visitation, followed by cremation, and burial the next day would be the plan.

I arrived early with the family on the day of the visitation, and when I saw Mary lying there, she could have been sleeping. She was absolutely radiant in her pink dress, and her hair and makeup were done to perfection. I thanked Michael for being so kind as to capture the real Mary. Everyone was amazed at her appearance. The flowers were beautiful, but the huge lump in my throat was all I could focus on. Tears flowed as we gazed upon her.

When the visitation started, I stood at Mary's casket and greeted the steady flow of friends and relatives who came by to pay their last respects.

I was touched when my former Palos Park neighbors, Don and Marcella appeared, along with their son Daryl, who was always Mary's favorite neighborhood kid. Even the staff of the Coralville Dam Army Corps of Engineers came by after seeing the notice in the newspaper. Mary and I worked as camp hosts for the Corps the previous summer, so it was special to me that they came by in uniform to pay their respects.

My relatives from Chicago came to Iowa for the services, as did some close friends and former neighbors. Two of our good friends even flew in from New Jersey and Texas to say their good-byes to Mary. It was heartening to me to see how many people loved that girl. C.J. Wright flew in and said the prayers at the visitation, and we had a harpist play as well.

There was only one awkward moment during the visitation, and it was a comment from a distant cousin of Mary's. To this day, I don't remember who it was, but it cut me to the quick. She came up to me, shook my hand, and offered her condolences. Then, out of the blue, said to me, "You're young; you'll marry again!" I was dumbstruck and did not know how to answer her at first. I looked down at my wedding ring and said, "That is the *last* thing on my mind right now." She just moved on and I then greeted the next person. The coldness of her statement still haunts me to this day, and, quite frankly, I can't understand what prompted her to say that. Did she think in some perverse way that a statement like that would comfort me? As if I was already horny and looking to get laid? I am still perplexed by it. That was just the first in a series of awkward statements that have been made to me over the past seven years.

It's been nearly seven years since Mary's passing, and I have had any number of odd comments made to me. Granted, most people feel awkward when speaking to a widow or widower. But I have come to the conclusion that a (relatively) young and good-looking man is expected to have a date on his arm soon after a loss, whereas, a widowed women is allowed to grieve. If she never has another date in her life, it is never questioned. But when it comes to men, only gray-haired old guys are allowed to grieve.

At the end of the visitation, the family said their tearful good-byes to Mary. Then it was my turn. I walked up to the open casket with Phyllis on one arm, and Janie on the other. As I drew near, I fell apart. It was the last time I would see her, and that realization hit me like a ton of bricks. I was sobbing uncontrollably, and had to be led out by my sisters-in-law, so I could compose myself. There have been few occasions in my life where I've been that emotional, and that had to be the worst of all. Saying good-bye to my lover, my best friend, my muse, my confidant, and the focus of my life for the past twenty-six years was very, very difficult.

The day of the funeral dawned; it was a beautiful, clear Iowa morning. The sun shone on fields of deep green corn and soybeans. What could be more perfect for giving an Iowa farmer's daughter a fond send-off? It could not have been more perfect.

We gathered at the Lensing Funeral Home at 9:00 a.m., C.J. said some closing prayers, and everyone filed past the walnut urn containing Mary's ashes to offer their good-byes one last time. We then got in the limousine and led the funeral cortege to the Monson farm. Kevin put up flags on poles at the entrance to their farm, and it reminded me of the narrow banners flown at a Renaissance Faire. We turned onto the drive from the paved road, and the magnificent red Monson barn loomed ahead about a half mile down their gravel drive.

The barn was all prepared for the services: a table was set up at the south door, Kevin's John Deere was there, and an expansive Iowa cornfield was in the background. It was absolutely perfect with a lone oak tree standing like a sentinel in the middle of the cornfield.

Chairs were set up theater-style for the many friends and family who attended. C.J. said a few inspiring words about her friend Mary, and then Dr. Rose's daughter sang "In My Life" and "Amazing Grace" beautifully. At this point, family members and friends got up to the podium, and spoke fondly of their memories of Mary.

The most touching ones came from her nieces and nephews, who spoke very openly about their favorite aunt. Mary's best friend, Linda Marie spoke of their childhood days, and being partners in crime. And one of the funniest moments was when Mary's old college friend Valorie told a story of their days together in college. Mary and Valorie missed a final exam, and unless they could retake the test, they would both have failed the class. She didn't even recall why they missed it, but she had fun telling us about Mary's solution to the problem. They had to meet with the professor to try and convince him to allow them to take the exam, and prior to entering the room Mary said, "Just let me do the talking." You must remember that this was in the early seventies, at the height of the drug culture that swept the nation's universities. When asked why they both missed their final exam, Mary calmly blurted out that they were arrested for possession of marijuana. The professor arranged for them to retake the test the next day, and both girls passed the course. Mary's hunch was right—the professor was a pothead, and her excuse carried more weight than any other she could fabricate. The crowd roared with laughter.

After the remembrances, people were asked to step outside into the Iowa sunshine, and a group of volunteers quickly turned the barn from a theater-style setting to a restaurant. The food was simple, but hot and delicious. People gathered in groups at tables inside the barn, and I went around and thanked everyone for coming. The consensus was that no one would have missed it for the world. My old buddy Ron came in from Chicago, and volunteered to drive my car in the funeral procession and bring my dog Austin along. Everyone got to meet our faithful cocker spaniel at Mary's funeral.

In the end, as I look back, I think I did everything I could—with the help of family and friends—to make Mary's final hours and her funeral, as perfect and as fitting as possible. She would have loved every aspect of it; I know it in my heart. From the beautiful pink dress she wore, to the barn and Kevin's tractor, to the water from the River Jordan that C.J. brought along to bless her ashes as they were interred on the farm the following day. I placed the ashes of our first cocker spaniel, Lady, in the grave with Mary's, and I plan to join them someday when I'm gone.

The agreement is this: our ashes will remain on the Jacobsen family farm until the day it's sold and no longer in the family. At that point, my nephew John Dennis, my trustee, will be charged with moving our remains to the cemetery in West Branch, along with the stone bench that has both our names engraved along with the phrase, "Traveling Together Forever."

EPILOGUE

Mary will always be a part of me.

Over seven years have passed since I lost my beloved to acute lymphocytic leukemia, a side effect of the treatment we hoped would save her life. It was one of the known risks of bone marrow transplantation that we accepted in hopes of a cure.

So much has changed since Mary's procedure in 1993, and advances in radiation and chemotherapeutic agents have mitigated much of the risk. It is my understanding that some bone marrow transplantation is being done on an outpatient basis. There is no longer a need for HEPA-filtrated isolation rooms.

People diagnosed with Hodgkin's disease and non-Hodgkin's lymphoma have reasons to be hopeful. Organizations like the Lymphoma Research Foundation are helping find a cure for this devastating disease. I hope everyone who reads this book will consider donating to this very worthy cause, and perhaps one day, people will not have to suffer like my Mary did.

Although time has healed some of the wounds, and as I move forward with the grieving process, I will always remember the wonderful times I shared with this remarkable woman, and I will love her forever. "Till Death do us part" meant something to me when I spoke those words on May 17, 1986, but my love for her and my duty as a husband did not end on July 8, 2006.

This book is my tribute to Mary, a celebration of a life well lived, and my final act of love. I will see you in my dreams, Sweetheart.

Killedguyedc.rr.com